M000217872

# Mule Musings

by: Basil Overton

*You May Get a "Kick" Out Of This Book,
And Detect Some "Stable" Reasoning While
You Do It.*

QUALITY PUBLICATIONS
P.O. BOX 1060
ABILENE, TEXAS 79604

© Basil Overton 1983

Use of cover illustration and illustrations on pages 12, 33, 72 and 93 by permisson of Bonnie Shields.

Use of photos on pages 11, 19, 26, 40, 50, 62, 108 and 120 by permission of Basil Overton.

ISBN:O-89137-105-2

## DEDICATION

To Billy and Gene, my brothers who were my plow partners, and fellow mule drivers and riders, when we were boys.

## BASIL OVERTON

From Weakley County, Tennessee -- Born 1925.

Has preached 38 years. Half these years in *mission* work.

Married to former Margie Medling.

Have been married 38 years.

Four children -- one deceased.

Freed-Hardeman -- 3 years -- was graduated with highest honors.

Abilene Christian -- 2 semesters

B. A. Degree -- Eastern Kentucky Univeristy

M. A. Degree -- University of Kentucky

Doctor's Degree -- Morehead State University (Doctor of Humanities)

Vice President and professor of Bible, Christian Evidences and Church History at International Bible College.

Editor of The World Evangelist which he started in 1972 -- about 50,000 regular paid circulation.

# Preface

The year is 1981. The headlines concern such things as space probes, moon trips, biogenetic engineering and the latest scandals of the "jet set." In the midst of such a world we are suddenly presented with a book of mule stories! In an age that has seen the passing of the steam locomotive and the introduction of nuclear power for daily use, is there also interest in mules and morality?

The astonishing answer is yes! In 1972 a newspaper style gospel journal was launched in Florence, Alabama, called *The World Evangelist*. While older papers of similar intent were sagging in circulation and many new ones were dying, *The World Evangelist* soared in circulation and in the appreciation of its readers. By far, the most popular article and (the one most quoted and discussed) was entitled "Mule Musings and Other Matters," written by the erudite editor, Basil Overton.

Dr. Overton is a man of wide ranging interests and an amazing record of accomplishments. In addition to his work as editor of *The World Evangelist* he also serves as Vice President of International Bible College and teaches overflowing classes in church history and Christian Evidences. He is an author with several books to his credit and is in great demand as a speaker. As this article is being prepared Dr. Overton is preaching every night in an evangelistic campaign at Killen, Alabama, and will also address the Alabama legislature this week as a spokesman for a citizens group concerned with better text books in the public schools.

Dr. Overton originated in the gently rolling hills of Western Tennessee where he learned to appreciate the wisdom and patience of the long-eared creatures he writes about. He travelled the world as a young sailor in World War II, and took his formal education in Tennessee, Texas and Kentucky.

Dr. Overton's hobby is gardening. His habits are scholarly. His disposition is as gentle and sunny as the rolling hills where he grew up. He walks daily in great reverence for God and with a world wide sympathy for fallible human beings who need God's grace.

It is out of this background of Tennessee farm boy, erudite scholar, busy editor, successful preacher, compassionate human being and Christian gentleman that Basil Overton has written his humorous and instructive "Mule Musings." He has chosen his subject well. Moses wrote about mules, and Jesus spoke of and rode animals of the same "kind." The book they helped to write has been a best seller for a long time!

The stories and lessons in *Mule Musings And Other Matters* have already proved their usefulness and reader appeal in *The World Evangelist*. In book form they will now be available to an ever growing number of delighted new readers as well as thousands of old friends who first read them in *The World Evangelist*.

Charles Coil, President
International Bible College
Florence, Alabama

## *Volume I*

# **Table of Contents**

# Introduction

## *Animals In The Bible*

Specific reference is made in the Bible to many animals, including fishes, birds, and insects. Often Biblical writers made reference to these to teach valuable lessons. Even the first chapter of the Bible which tells us of God's great work of creation, gives considerable attention to moving creatures, fowl, great whales, cattle, beasts of the earth and everything that creepeth. The entire Old Testament abounds in references to the creatures of the animal kingdom. Every child thrills at hearing the story of the flood and the animals entering the ark.

Reference is often made to animals in that beautiful and practical book of poetry known as Proverbs. In Chapter 30 the following are mentioned: ravens, eagles, serpents, ants, conies, locusts, the spider, a lion, and a greyhound.

Often Biblical writers bore down heavily upon the foolish and disobedient. For an example, Solomon said an indiscreet but beautiful woman is like a jewel of gold in a hogs nose! (Proverbs 11:22).

The little ant is used in the Bible as an illustration of industry and dependability and to show God's disapproval of laziness. "Go to the ant, thou sluggard; consider her ways, and be wise" (Proverbs 6:6). Indeed, the Bible abounds with references to animals to teach us important lessons.

Isaiah recorded that God Almighty said of his disobedient children whom he had nourished and brought up, and who had rebelled against him, that they were not acting as smart as an ox or an ass, because he said, "The ox knoweth his owner, and the ass his master's crib, but Israel doth not know, my people doth not consider." (Isaiah 1:2,3).

The New Testament also abounds with references to members of the animal kingdom. If anyone thinks that reference to such should be considered as being beneath the dignity of one who teaches God's word let him take a close look at the teaching of Jesus the Master Teacher who in his teaching frequently referred to creatures of the animal kingdom to teach great lessons that had to do with the souls and the eternal destiny of people. Jesus referred to moths, fowl, dogs, hogs, fish, serpents, vipers, foxes, sheep, wolves, camels, gnats, hens, chickens, and others.

Jesus said that some of God's people of his time did not act as wisely as little chickens (Matthew 23:37). James taught that horses and other animals could be tamed, but, that the human tongue could not be tamed (James 3). One can so train some mules that they can be directed without the restraint of a bridle. You can take the bridle off a tamed mule but never should the bridle be taken from the tongue! The tongue is never that tamed, so said James by the Holy Spirit!

Stories and illustrations about mules abound. Some of these stories and illustrations contain a species of humor. But even our Lord used some humor. He was humorous when he pictured the mote hunter, and asked how one could get the mote (small particle of trash) out of his brother's eye when he had a beam (a large object) in his own eye (Matthew 7:1-5). Our Lord virtually was asking, "How can you get a piece of broom straw out of your brother's eye, when you have a broom handle in your own eye?" He obviously meant that one with many sins should not try to pick out the little faults of others until he has corrected his own faults.

The Lord was also humorous, and yet administered a strong rebuke when he said, "Ye blind guides, which strain out the gnat and swallow the camel" (Matthew 23:24). He probably alluded to the milking of a camel where one saw a gnat in the milk and hastily filtered such an unclean creature out. No one could literally swallow a camel, but the lesson the Lord taught was concerning the inconsistency of the Jews who were greatly concerned over some small matters but not at all concerned about weightier matters.

In his *Essa on the Muel* (Essay on the Mule), the great humorist, Josh Billings, said of mules: "Tha are like sum men, verry korrupt at harte; ive known them tu be good muels for six months, just to git a good chanse to kick sumbody." This is strong satire, and sounds a warning regarding how dangerous some people are!

Josh Billings expressed doubt in his "essa" that the Bible referred to mules, but it does refer to them many times. In a sense a mule hanged a disobedient son of a king. When at the terrible battle of the Wood of Ephraim, Absalom who had betrayed king David his own father, was riding a mule, and the mule went under the thick boughs of a great oak, and Absalom's head caught in the oak and he was suspended "be tween the heaven and the earth; and the mule that was under him went away." His mule forsook him and left him hanging later to be killed by the darts and blows of his enemies. (2 Samuel 18). Thus a mule played an important role in the fate of one who rebelled against constituted authority.

David is mentioned by name more in the Bible than

any other man. The Bible also says king David had a mule, and that shortly after he died, his son Solomon, rode on that mule on his way to sit on the throne of God in the place of his father (1 Kings 1:38, 46; 1 Chronicles 29: 23).

Our King, the Lord Jesus, rode triumphantly into Jerusalem upon an animal that was of the same *kind* as a mule. "Tell ye the daughter of Zion, Behold thy King cometh unto thee, meek, and sitting upon an ass, and a colt the foal of an ass." (Matthew 21:5).

**Charles Coil (left) and Basil Overton with mules that were owned by Wayne Gean.**

## "I've Always Wanted To"

An interesting story has come out of the West about a prospector. The prospector came riding into town on his faithful mule, and when he got off his mule the town bully began to shoot into the ground around the prospector's feet and to tell him to dance. The prospector said, "I don't dance." The bully insisted that he dance anyway as he kept shooting around the treasure hunter's feet. Finally the victim of the bully's abuse began to dance a little, and about that time the bully ran out of shells in his pistol. Whereupon the prospector pulled out of a saddle bag a big, long pistol and pointed it in the face of the bully and said, "Did you ever kiss a mule?" The bully answered, "No, but I've always wanted to!"

I suppose one would kiss a mule if sufficiently motivated! But just think of what we can do in the cause of our Lord, if we are sufficiently motivated. We should be motivated to serve Christ zealously and faithfully by just thinking about how bad off we were when we were not Christians and how blessed we are in Christ. The New Testament epistles emphasize this contrast in many places. For an example: "That at that time ye were without Christ, being aliens from the commonwealth of Israel, and strangers from the covenants of promise, having no hope, and without God in the world: but now in Christ Jesus ye who sometimes were far off are made nigh by the blood of Christ." (Ephesians 2:12,13). What greater motivation could one need than to reflect on what and where he was before becoming a Christian, and then think about how wonderful it is to be in Christ?

We should be greatly motivated by the love of Christ. "For the love of Christ constraineth us." (2 Cor-

13

inthians 5:14). Knowing how Christ loves us should move us to faithfully serve him without having to be begged to serve him.

## Indecisiveness

The story is told of a mule that died of starvation because he would not make up his mind about which of two haystacks he would go to eat. He started toward one, then turned toward the other only to turn back to the first stack he saw. It has been reported that he did this until he starved trying to make up his mind.

I do not believe this story because I know mules too well. I believe any mule that has ever lived was too smart to be so indecisive. If the story had been about a human, I might believe it, for I have seen some humans that had great difficulty making up their minds, thinking one way, then another, and seeming to have great difficulty in making up their minds.

James wrote that, "A double minded man is unstable in all his ways" (James 1:8). The Greek word James used which is translated *double minded* is the word *dipsuchos* (di su kos), and it is defined: "double minded, inconstant, fickle." Of course the Holy Spirit through James did not mean a man literally has two minds, but a fickle person acts as if he has two minds. "Double minded" is somewhat like "two faced." It is reported that a person said to another, "I heard you are two faced, but you really are not, are you?" The reply was, "No." Whereupon the inquirer said, "I just knew you were not two faced, because I felt that if you were, you would not wear the face you have but the other one." Have you ever felt this way about a double minded person? You might have doubted he was double minded because if he were he surely would not keep on using the one he was using!

## Risking His Neck

When driving on a Kentucky highway one day, I saw a mule standing in grass up to his knees with his neck pressed hard against a barbed wire fence. He was reaching as far as he could to graze in the same kind of grass in which he was standing. I wondered why the mule was risking getting his neck cut or scratched on the fence because he could have eaten in the luscious grass in which he was standing and thereby have avoided the pain and danger of the barbed wire!

I suppose we should expect a mule to engage in such strange conduct. However, we humans with all our brains and sense seem to act no better than that mule. History is filled with stories of people who risked not merely receiving pain and injury, but even their lives, trying to get something that was really no better than what they already had. Many have injured their health, and some have lost their lives seeking in a greedy manner to acquire more of what they already abundantly possessed. Epicurus felt that wealth did not consist in having so many great possessions as much as it consisted in having few wants! Another has said that true wealth is having the ability to be content with little!

Do not fret; do not risk your neck just for the sake of acquiring more and more of what you may already have in abundance! "For godliness with contentment is great gain. For we brought nothing into this world, and it is certain we can carry nothing out. And having food and raiment let us be therewith content. But they that will be rich fall into temptation and a snare, and into many foolish and hurtful lusts, which drown men in destruction and perdition. For the love of money is the root of all evil: which while some coveted after, they have erred from the faith and pierced themselves through with many sorrows" (1 Timothy 6:6-10).

## Paying For Madness And Folly

A farm magazine reported that a farmer was having difficulty getting his mules to come to the barn from the pasture. He ran them around over the pasture a number of times and seeing they seemed so determinded not to go to the barn, he became so enraged he decided to shoot them. He went to his house in a rage and found his shot gun. While he looked for the shells in a bureau drawer, he found the mortgage on the mules! The mortgage reminded him of what he owed on the mules and his rage and madness subsided somewhat as he thought about having to pay for the mules after their deaths. He decided not to shoot the critters. The mortgage saved the mules!

What a lesson! So many spend their lives paying for their madness and folly. While enraged one can easily say and/or do things for which he may have to pay a high price as long as he lives. Even if one is forgiven by the heavenly Father and cleansed of his iniquity he may still have to pay a high price for the folly of his madness. "Be ye angry and sin not: let not the sun go down upon your wrath: neither give place to the devil" (Ephesians 4:26,27). If you are prone to become angry easily, you should pray that something will happen to cause your anger to subside before you do something foolish like shooting your mules! You had better hope you find the mortgage while looking for the shells!

Our sins, whether committed in madness or calmness can have long lingering consequencs. A young man who had lived a dissolute life was asked if he was still getting a kick out of his sinful way of living. He solemnly replied, "No, but I'm getting a kickback!" The kickback of sin always comes. "For he that soweth to his flesh shall of the flesh reap corruption" (Galatians 6:8).

"Patch," a horse mule (male) lives by Mars Hill Rd. in Florence, Ala. about two miles from my office. He is owned by Edsel May. I stopped to see "Patch" recently and his master told me he plows his big garden with him. I found Edsel to be a cordial host and learned that "Patch" is of gentle disposition. I know some people who could learn from him in this respect.

— The Author

19

## When There Is Nothing To Fear

My Dad, W. R. Overton, (deceased) told me he once had great difficulty trying to get his mules into the barn. The mules seemed determined not to go into the barn. Finally Dad tucked a sheet under his arm and walked quietly to the back of the pasture to a place where his mules could not see him. He unfolded the white sheet and spread it over himself and started walking toward his mules and began waving his arms under the sheet. When the mules saw him they were overcome with terror and made a sudden getaway toward the barn.

My Dad felt good that his trick had worked so well and he walked to the barn to close the doors of the stables where he confidently expected to find the stubborn mules. He was truly surprised to discover that the mules were not in their stables. He began to investigate and discovered that the mules had gone over the barnyard fence! He found them halted before a gate that kept them from completely leaving his premises and entering a wide open world!

My Dad's mules remind me of people that get excited and "jump fences" so to speak when there is really nothing over which to be excited. I have thought how amusing it would have been had those mules gone up to my Dad and with their mouths pulled that sheet off of him! Many times people need to investigate that over which they become so excited and about which they may get "carried away." Not everything that looks frightening is really dangerous. Of course one can go to the other extreme and not be excited over real dangers, or not be aware of dangers at all. But it is lamentable that some even in the church seem to always be sensing danger in what others in the church may do. Some are so afraid they will do wrong by do-ing something that they may not do right! One can be so afraid to do things for the Lord he may not do anything. And doing nothing is really frightening! There is nothing more unscriptural than doing nothing!

The servant who received one talent from his lord was afraid when there was nothing to fear. He said to his lord: "And I was afraid, and went and hid thy talent in the earth: lo there thou hast that is thine" (Matthew 25:25). The Psalmist described some as: "There were they in great fear, where no fear was"(Psalms 53:5).

## She Did Not Want A Divorce

I heard about a woman who felt her husband was oppressing her and she went to the judge about it. She told the judge she felt her husband was not working enough and that he was making her do too much of the work. She said, "Judge, he makes me pull a plow along with a mule." The judge replied, "I don't blame you if you want a divorce." She said, "You misunderstand, Judge, I do not want to divorce my husband; I just want you to make him get a mule that will pull his part."

Whether the foregoing really happened or not, I'm unable to say. But I am in position to say with a degree of certainty that there are some husbands who do little work compared to what their wives do; and they seem not to care how hard their wives have to work. A wife should expect to do her part of the work necessary to the maintaining of a household or a family. But, the husband should accept the responsibility of being the principal one to labor and provide for his family. The man who is able to work and will not provide for his family is worse than an infidel (1 Timothy 5:8). The Holy Spirit guided Paul to write "that if any would not work, neither should he eat" (2 Thessalonians 3:10). In the next verse Paul said that those in the church who worked not at all were walking disorderly. He also said Christians are to withdraw from all who walk disorderly. This means if a member of the church will not work, the church should not only *not support him*, but it should withdraw from him!

Someone has reported that a man went to his doctor and after an examination and interview with the doctor, he said, "Give it to me straight, doc. I can take it! Tell me in plain English what's the matter with me."

22

The doctor said, "All right, I'll be frank with you. My diagnosis is that you are just plain lazy!" The patient replied, "All right , doc, please give me a scientific name for it so I can go home and tell my wife."

## Behe

Behe was the name of a mule Charlie Benson, a great uncle of mine owned. It was reliably reported to me that while pulling a plow, Behe would stop when an airplane flew over, and he would look up at the airplane. Mules are very observant creatures, but Behe is the only mule I ever heard of that would look up at airplanes!

We humans should be very observant; we should know what is going on around us. "See that ye walk circumspectly, not as fools, but as wise" (Ephesians 5:15). *Circumspectly* in this verse means looking all around. Christians are to be vigilant because the devil is after them (1 Peter 5:8).

The story is told of a fire that was burning in a hotel room. Firemen finally got the door open, rushed in and found a man in bed asleep in the burning room. They awoke him and got him outside the room and one asked him why he went to bed smoking a cigarette, He said, "I didn't, I don't smoke." He was then asked: "Well how did the fire get started?" He replied: "I don't know, it was burning when I went to bed."

You might say, "Surely, that is just a story; nobody would be that unobservant." You are probably right. But, we can be unobservant and unaware of spiritual dangers that could be even more dangerous than a fire in a room. "Beware lest any man spoil you through philosophy and vain deceit, after the tradition of men, after the rudiments of the world, and not after Christ" (Colossians 2:8).

## Paying Attention

Reeder Allen, a long time friend of mine told me about an experience with his boys when they were much younger. He bought a mule and told his boys he wanted them to learn to plow and make a garden. He instructed them and finally one day before he left to go to work he told his boys to plow some or be ready to plow when he got home that afternoon. When he got home the boys felt they were ready to plow. They had the mule's collar on bottom side up, and the gear on backwards! Evidently the boys did not listen too well to their daddy's instruction.

Wouldn't it be great if people just failed to pay attention to such little matters as how to put a mule to a plow! But, some children as well as some adults are not giving proper attention to matters that pertain to their welfare in this world, as well as their eternal destiny in the world to come! Failing to pay attention to what one needs to hear can cause him many miseries in this life, and can cause one to be lost eternally.

Most of us are like the Psalmist who said, "Lord, hear my voice: let thine ears be attentive to the voice of my supplications" (Psalms 130:2). *Attentive* in this verse is from the Hebrew word *Kawshab* which is defined: "to prick up the ears; to give heed; to regard." Indeed, we want God to "prick up his ears" to pay close attention to us, but we are not as anxious to "prick up our ears" to listen to what God tells us in his word. "Therefore, we ought to give the more earnest heed to the things we have heard, lest at any time we should let them slip" (Hebrews 2:1).

Because Jesus was teaching daily in the temple, the very religious Jewish leaders sought to destroy him,

"And could not find what they might do: for all the people were very attentive to hear him" (Luke 19:48). What these were doing is literally expressed in the Greek as, "They were hanging on him listening."

Do you pay close attention when in an assembly and a preacher is preaching the gospel? If you love the truth it won't be so easy for you to be detracted. Here is a conversation that illustrates what I mean.

"George, did you notice the handsome fur coat worn by the young lady in front of us in church today?"

"No my dear, I'm afraid I didn't. In fact, I think I was dozing most of the time."

"Indeed! A lot of good it does you to go to church."

## Cannot Defy Gravity

I remember about thiry-five years ago that the champion lie told in the National Lying Contest was as follows: A man reported that he was riding his mule and he and the mule went over a cliff and fell about 500 feet. Someone told the man if that were true he and the mule could not have survived. The man replied: "Neither the mule nor I was injured; I just held back real tight on the reins and we went down easy."

The reason the foregoing is funny is because everybody knows that the one who told it knew that everybody would know it was untrue.

However, there are those telling lies today as if they were true! One cannot defy gravity even when riding a mule! For that reason anybody knows he cannot ride a mule over a cliff without injury or death. But some seem to think they can defy laws of God relative to moral conduct and not be injured or die. But they cannot. The so-called "New Morality" is a lie that is being told as though it were the truth. It is not new at all! It is the old immorality with a new name. Those who believe it are defying God's laws and will suffer. "Be not deceived; God is not mocked; for whatsoever a man soweth, that shall he also reap" (Galatians 6:7).

The champion lie mentioned above is humorous. The lie of "the new morality" is not humorous. This deceitful philosophy has damned many souls. It has wrecked many homes. It has broken many hearts.

The so-called "New morality" leads some people to think it is all right for them to do whatever they want to do.

"There is a way which seemeth right unto a man, but the end thereof are the ways of death" (Proverbs 14:12).

Even if a person thinks what he does is all right, but it is really transgression of God's word, it is sin. Sin is sin, and has its awful consequences whether we recognize it as such or not.

"For the wages of sin is death; but the gift of god is eternal life through Jesus Christ our Lord" (Romans 6:23).

Many go over the "cliffs" of transgression and disobedience, perhaps thinking they will be let down easy, but they land hard!

"Good understanding giveth favor: but the way of transgressors is hard" (Proverbs 13:15).

## "He Got Religion"

James Griffith of Walker County, Alabama told me a true story. A family farmed an island in Warrior River. In order to do so they had to use a flatboat to get to the island and carrry their mule and farming equipment to the island and back. One day when the boat docked, the mule got contrary and would not get off the boat.

The boys doing the farming tried to get the mule to leave the boat. He finally backed into the water and almost drowned. The boys reported the incident to their mother and she asked, "Wonder what was wrong?" The youngest boy said, "I believe he got religion and wanted to be baptized."

Obviously, the mule did not get religion and desire to be baptized. However, what the boy said is no more contrary to what the Bible teaches about baptism than what some preachers say about baptism.

1. Some preachers say baptism is not essential to salvation. But the Bible says it is (Mark 16:16; Acts 2:38; Acts 22; 1 Peter 3:21). Some preachers regularly teach "He that believeth and is *not* baptized shall be saved." But, Jesus said, "He that believeth and *is* baptized shall be saved."

2. Some preachers teach that a few drops of water poured, or sprinkled on a person's head is just as good as one's being immersed in water. But, "baptism" means "immersion." This is obvious in view of the fact that Paul said being baptized involves being buried (Romans 6:4; Colossians 2:12).

3. Some preachers say infants are fit subjects of baptism. But, Bible baptism was for believers who repented of their sins and confessed Christ. An infant has no sins from which to turn and is not aware of sin, and cannot believe, repent, or confess.

Yes, what the young man on Warrior River said about the mule being baptized is just as scriptural as some things that some preachers say about baptism.

## Some Do Not Reason Well

The story is told that some men were trying to get a mule to go into a barn and the mule's ears were extra long. (A mule is sensitive about his ears.) His ears kept striking against a beam that hanged rather low over the entrance, and he refused to go through the door. Finally, the men decided to jack up the barn. While they were in the process of doing so, someone suggested they dig out the ground under the entrance enough that the mule could go in. One of the men replied: "It's his ears that are too long, not his legs."

The foregoing reply illustrates a very obvious fact, and that is, some people do not reason very well, This seems to be especially true in religious matters. It has been the observation of this writer that many use good judgment in most everything except religion. For an example it is not even reasonable that the Lord would foster and promote a number of religious doctrines which contradict each other. Most anyone would censure and condemn a man who claimed to be guided by the Lord in his teaching but constantly taught contradictory doctrines. However, it is obvious that many of the same people would not censure preachers who claim to be guided by the Lord but contradict each other in their teaching.

Jesus prayed that all who believe on him through God's word would be one, even as he and the Father are one (John 17:8, 21). This surely was a reasonable prayer.

## He Paid Me A Nickel

When I was a boy, one day a neighbor's mules got out of their fenced bounds and went on a rather extended adventure. The neighbor asked me to go with him in trying to get the mules back in their fenced-in home. We followed the mules several miles before we were able to get control of them and bring them back to their proper place. They went through fields, briars, thickets and down the public road. We really had quite a chore getting them back. They went almost to the city limits of the closest town.

I remember that the neighbor gave me a nickel for helping him get back his mules. I was not expecting any money for the arduous task. A nickel was big money to me then! However, we were taught at home not to expect money or pay for everything we did. We six children grew up under the influence of the philosophy that one was supposed to do things for his neighbors and without expecting to be paid for every deed done. We worked for neighbors for pay, but there were some things we did for which we did not expect pay.

It is a sad sign when children grow up expecting to be paid money for everything they do. It seems that many children are being reared with this concept. It is a concept that is not conducive to proper education and development. The most precious things in life cannot be obtained with money, and one of these things is the spirit of helpfulness and good neighborliness. The spirit of unselfishness and willingness to help others just for the sake of being helpful cannot be measured in terms of money.

"Love worketh no ill to his neighbor, therefore, love is the fulfilling of the law" (Romans 13:10).

## A Story By Abraham Lincoln

I took my wife and two daughters to Washington. We visited many of the interesting places. One of the most touching experiences one can have if he knows about Abraham Lincoln is to visit The Lincoln Memorial near the banks of the Potomac in the capital city.

It has been said more has been written about Abraham Lincoln than any other person except Jesus of Nazareth. And yet, Jesus was born in a barn, and Lincoln was born in a house that was not nearly as good a building as most barns.

Abraham Lincoln had "the common touch." He was a wise giver of advice. Men sought his counsel in settling their troubles. It is reported that on one occasion when he practiced law in Springfield, Illinois two men who were having a dispute came to his office at noon and asked him to settle their fuss. He said, "Sit down and wait; when I return from lunch I'll help you. He locked the door as he went out and did not return until evening. When he returned the two men had settled the dispute themselves!

But, one of the good stories about Lincoln involved a mule. Lincoln appointed men of opposite parties to important places of work. In one case, two such men were not getting along well, but each was doing his job well. However, some critic complained to Lincoln because the two men were not getting along. Lincoln told the critic a story. He said a man was plowing with a mule; someone came along and while "visiting" the man who was plowing, he noticed a horsefly on the mule, and attempted to kill the pesky fly. The plowman said: "Don't kill that fly; that fly is all that keeps the mule going!"

34

If there are irritating things in life, just count them as good reasons for going right on doing right and serving God. Henry Ward Beecher said, "Troubles are the tools by which God fashions us for better things...Difficulties are God's errands and trainers, and only through them can one come to the fulness of manhood." Epictetus said, "Difficulties are things that show what men are." James, a servant of God and of the Lord Jesus Christ, said, "My brethren, count it all joy when ye fall into divers temptations; knowing this, that the trying of your faith worketh patience" (James 1:2,3). *Temptations* in this text is translated from Greek peirasmois. One of the definitions of the singular form of this word is: "a putting to the proof; a trial." Likely, this is what James meant.

I like the observation about a mule that a school boy made; he said, "A mule is a heartier bird than a goose or a turkey, and is different. He wears his wings on his head. He has four legs to walk with, and he is awfully backward about going forward."

## "Whoa" and Woe

Charles Coil told me about a mule that posed a problem for the person riding him. When the mule ran and the rider would say "Whoa," the mule would stop so suddenly, the rider would go over the mule's head and hit the ground several feet ahead of the mule. Someone asked the mule's owner why the mule did this. The owner said the mule used to be in the habit of not stopping at all when one said "Whoa!" So he had trained the mule to stop when he said, "Whoa!" He had trained the mule by putting a sack over his head and turning him around several times so he would lose his sense of direction. Then the owner would get on the mule and ride toward the barn. When the mule reached a rapid pace the owner would yell, "Whoa!" The mule would not stop, but the owner would jump off and the mule would run head-on into the barn because the sack was over his eyes. The owner said that after two or three "applications" of this treatment the mule would come to a sudden halt when told to "Whoa!"

That mule would have been much better off had he stopped when one said "Whoa!" He could have avoided that running into the barn! He learned the hard way what he needed to do!

That mule was no different in one way to some humans. Some people seem determined to learn everything the hard way! They ignore the fact that others have already "run into the barn" because they would not listen to wise direction. The Lord, so to speak, says "Whoa!" But too often people do not stop when God says "Whoa!" They learn the hard way that they should have stopped. It is a pity that people do not realize that God has good reasons for saying "Whoa" to us.

Often young children think they know more than their parents. They refuse the wise instruction of their parents. They pay no attention to their parents when they say "Whoa!" (Proverbs 1:8)

"A fool despiseth his father's instruction: but he that regardeth reproof is prudent" (Proverbs 15:5).

God knows that our doing some things is not good for us. God's restrictions on our lives were designed in his infinite wisdom for our benefit. It is too bad that every generation seems determined to learn the hard way that, "Good understanding giveth favour: but the way of transgressors is hard" (Proverbs 13:15).

Here is a good "Whoa" that many ignore and thereby get into serious trouble and bring woe and grief upon others. "Wine is a mocker, strong drink is raging: and whosoever is deceived thereby is not wise" (Proverbs 20:1).

Another "Whoa" that brings *woe* if ignored is, "A foolish woman is clamorous: she is simple and knoweth nothing. For she sitteth at the door of her house, on a seat in the high places of the city to call passengers who go right on their ways: whoso is simple, let him turn in hither:and as for him that wanteth understanding, she saith to him, stolen waters are sweet, and bread eaten in secret is **pleasant**. But he knoweth not that the dead are there; and that her guests are in the depths of hell" (Proverbs 9:13-18). Of the same kind of promiscous woman, the same wise man sounded a "Whoa" when he said, "Hearken unto me now therefore, O ye children, and attend to the words of my mouth. Let not thine heart decline to her ways; go not astray to the words of my mouth. Let not thine heart decline to her ways; go not astray in her paths. For she hath cast down many wounded: yea, many strong men have been slain by her. Her house is the way to hell, going down to the chambers of  death; (Proverbs 7:24-27).

Thank you, Charles for the mule story; maybe it will remind some people to listen and stop when God says "Whoa!"

Failing to stop when God says "Whoa!" can make you wish you had run into a barn instead of doing what you did!

## Remaining Calm

Near where I was born there lived two men. One was named Willie, and the other's name was Elbert. Elbert's mules frequently got out of their pasture and transgressed on Willie's property. Finally Willie captured the mules and when Elbert came after them Willie "cussed" him for not keeping his mules in their proper place better. He severely "cussed" him, and while he "cussed" him, Elbert was packing tobacco into his pipe. When Willie stopped "cussing" Elbert gently and softly said, "Willie, you got a match?" This was his response to the "cussing." While I do not encourage the habit of smoking a pipe, I must admit that Elbert's response to such a bitter harangue manifested a splendid attitude. The wise man said, "A soft answer turneth away wrath" (Proverbs 15:1). How true!

If you can speak kindly in response to one who has spoken abusively to you, you possess a great characteristic; you wield a tremendous force. While I do not know the sequel to the Willie - Elbert drama, I do know that replying courteously to one who has spoken harshly to you will no doubt result in good, whereas if one responds to a "cussing" with a "cussing" he is not apt to do any good, and will usually only make matters worse.

I heard of one man who called another by a very course and crude title. Whereupon the victim responded: "No, you are wrong, I am not what you have called me. I am a Christian, but I want to give you a word of warning. Sometime you may call someone what you have called me and he may be just what you have called me! If he is, you will really be in trouble; he may kill you!"

If you are a Christian, and someone should speak

harshly to you, you do not have to smoke a pipe and ask him for a match. Instead, ask him if he believes in God? Or, invite him to attend worship with you. "For by thy words thou shalt be justified, and by thy words thou shalt be condemned" (Matthew 12:37). The way you respond to the man who speaks harshly to you could determine his eternal destiny as well as your own eternal destiny!

## Taking Advantage

A few days ago while driving on a country road not far from where I live I saw a scene that amused me and also bothered me. Someone had put a pile of hay in a pasture where there was a mule, a horse, and a cow. The mule had taken charge of all the hay! He had his ears laid back on the back of his head which was a sure sign he might start kicking any moment! He was shifting with rapid motion his kicking apparatus in the direction of the cow, then in the direction of the horse. This repeated shifting action, and his ears laid low, seemed to be sufficient warning to the cow and the horse, both of which seemed settled on letting the mule have all the hay rather than risk encountering the mule's hard kicking back legs and feet.

I was amused at this scene because a mule amuses me. I am especially amused when a mule exercises his prowess and demonstrates his unique ability. However, this mule-o-drama bothered me because the mule was taking advantage of the cow and the horse, and I hate to see even an animal mistreated.

Such a scene saddens me more when I think of the greed so common in the hearts of people. That mule did not act as bad as some people act. The mule was not as dangerous in his greed as some people are in their greed and avarice.

Not only are some people greedy; they are abusive and destructive in their greed. "He that is greedy of grain troubleth his own house" (Proverbs 15:27). Paul wrote of some, "who being past feeling have given themselves over unto lasciviousness to work all uncleanness with greediness" (Ephesians 4:19). You may have wondered why some who were greedy could act so badly. The answer is: they were past feeling!

When one who is greedy has no compunction of conscience, he can bring upon others much woe. However, a greedy person can also pull down on himself a world of woe.

The word in the Greek text of Ephesians 4:19 translated *greediness* is *pleonexia*. The Greeks defined this word as "the accursed love of possessing." This word describes the man who is set on getting in his greed what he wants: He does not care who he hurts and what methods he may employ as long as he gets what he wants!

Beware of greed! A greedy human can do much more harm than a greedy, kicking mule!

## "He Didn't Look Good"

Bill Swetmon heard a mule story and sent it to me. It is reported that a farmer bought a mule from a neighbor. Soon the farmer took the mule back to that neighbor and said, "This mule you sold me is almost blind." The neighbor replied, "I told you before you bought that mule that he was a fine mule but didn't *look* too good."

What that neighbor said about that mule was misleading. Evidently he deliberately deceived with that statement. Lies can sound so true!

The above mule story reminds me of the man who sold a cow. He told the buyer that the cow gave oodles of milk. That evening the new owner milked the cow and got only a teacup full of milk. He was quite disturbed but decided that moving the cow to her new home might have caused her to give just a little milk. He also thought the former owner might have milked the cow shortly before she made the trip to her new home. The new owner hoped for more milk the next morning.

The next morning the man milked the cow again but still got just a teacup full. He was enraged; he went to the former owner and said to him: "You told me that cow gave oodles of milk. What did you mean by oodles of milk"? The former owner replied, "About enough for your coffee."

Everyone should always speak the truth and never deliberately leave a misleading conception of that about which he has spoken. Winston Churchill referred to lying as "terminological inexactitude."

One can mislead without intending to do so. Poor punctuation and sentence structure can be quite misleading. For an example a preacher tried to tell of

43

the death of a drunken woman and he said it like this: "A young woman in my neighborhood died very suddenly last Sunday, while I was preaching the gospel in a state of beastly intoxication."

A person meant to convey the following message to a minister: "A man having gone to sea, his wife desires the prayers of the congregation for his safety." However, his poor spelling and punctuation caused him to write: "A person having gone to see his wife, desires the prayers of the congregation for his safety."

Do your best not to mislead unintentionally. By all means do not mislead people intentionally.

"Lie not one to another" (Colossians 3:9)

## "Lofty" Humor!

Jess Carter told me about something that happened in Okmulgee County, Oklahoma. Some boys played a prank on a man. They took bales of hay from his barn loft and made them into stairsteps and led the man's mule up the steps into the loft. Then they put the hay back into the loft.

When the mule's owner came to feed the mule he wondered where the animal was. He finally learned that his faithful beast was enjoying a feast of hay in the barn loft. He studied about it for some time, wondering how the mule could have climbed the ladder on the wall into the loft. He was really and truly baffled!

Finally, one of the boy pranksters came along and the man expressed his bewilderment over how his mule got into the loft. Also, he told the boy he just did not know how he was going to get the mule out of the loft!

The young man suggested that they stack the bales of hay so as to form steps on which the mule could descend to the ground. This they did, but the man seemed never to realize that such a system of hay bale stairsteps was the way the mule ascended into the loft!

This story illustrates the sense of humor of perhaps a majority of boys. Not all boys are as clever as the ones who built the stairway to a barn loft out of bales of hay. Perhaps this prank did no harm, but boys, and all people, should be careful not to do things as pranks which are of a destructive and harmful nature.

The foregoing story also illustrates how some do not sense what is so very obvious. It seems the baffled and bewildered owner of the mule would have readily realized how his beast got into the barn loft.

Not all people possess an equal amount of perceptive

power, but some seem not to discipline themselves to be as perceptive as they could be. One should train himself to be alert and train his reasoning powers. Some seem to be mentally lazy and do not use their mental ability as well as they could.

It has been estimated that only about fifteen per cent of the average mind is used.

Some are without excuse in their failure to perceive matters that are obvious. Paul wrote of some who turned away from God even though they were surrounded by the things that were made by God. He said they were without excuse. (Romans 1:20)

The Jews heard Jesus and saw his mighty works, yet most of them rejected him. The things that should have been easily perceived by them to be obvious evidences of his being the Messiah seemed to cause them to reject him. Jesus said they were "thick headed," or their hearts were waxed gross. (Matthew 13:14,15) They did not exercise their perceptive powers!

## Mule Riders

Riding mules has been long practiced. Riding a mule was one of the treats of my boyhood days. The word of God says King David had a mule to ride. (1 Kings 1:33) His sons rode mules. (2 Samuel 13:29) One of them, Absalom, was riding a mule during his rebellious action against his father, and "the mule went under the thick boughs of a great oak, and his head caught hold of the oak, and he was taken up between the heaven and the earth; and the mule that was under him went away" (2 Samuel 18:9). Absalom was in quite a predicament when his mule went away! Ten of Joab's armour bearers surrounded the scene when Absalom hanged between heaven and earth and they killed him. (2 Samuel 18:15)

Mules no doubt helped the Jews greatly in their return from Babylonian captivity for among their great number of animals there were 245 mules. (Ezra 2:66)

One story of mule riding teaches a timely lesson. A man was riding a mule and his wife was walking a few feet behind, Someone pointed toward the man's wife and asked him, "Why ain't she ridin'?" The man on the mule replied, "She ain't got no mule."

Obviously, the man on the mule was very inconsiderate of his wife. Too often marriage partners are not as thoughtful of each other as they should be. The man on the mule evidently had about the same conception of what a wife is as a man in the following story. It is reported that a man went to an under-developed country and when he returned home he was telling of some of the quaint conditions and customs of the country he had visited. He said, among other things, that in that country a wife cost five dollars. One of his listeners retorted: "Well, a good wife is worth five dollars."

Most marriage problems could be eliminated if both husband and wife would be considerate and thoughtful of each other. "Wives, submit yourselves unto your own husbands, as unto the Lord" (Ephesians 5:22). "Husbands, love your wives, even as Christ also loved the church, and gave himself for it" (Ephesians 5:25). Paul told Titus to teach the aged women to teach the young women to love their husbands (Titus 2:4). True love means being considerate and thoughtful of the one loved.

Husbands, let's get down off our mules, so to speak, and let our wives ride. Let's be more considerate of them, for what Lord Byron said of a good wife is indeed true. He said she is "The rainbow in the storms of life." John Milton said of the good wife, "She is heaven's last best gift."

Wife, be considerate of your husband. What kind of a wife are you? Do you do most of the talking in the home? Someone said a husband is a man of a few words? If this describes your husband, is it your fault? Are you considerate of him as the head of the house?

It is reported that a man died and someone asked one of his boys, "What were your paw's last words?" The boy replied, "He did not have any, maw was there."

## Boasting

My father, W.R. Overton, told me about buying a mule from a brother in the Lord. Before buying the mule, the brother and Dad were observing the mule, a horse, and some cows in a pasture. The brother sincerely boasted about what a good mule he had and along with other nice things he said about the mule, "That mule won't bother cows." Soon thereafter, the horse went to the barn, and the mule began to bother the cows. He ran after them until the cows jumped over the fence! The good brother was stunned; he said to Dad, "I just stood here and told you that mule would not bother cows." The brother was honest; he had not tried to deceive Dad. He had bragged on the mule, really thinking the mule would not bother cows. But, you can't always tell what a mule will do. In that respect they are somewhat like people.

Have you ever boasted about your child, and then the child did something to prove you were not so sure of what you had said? Maybe you have spoken highly of some person, even a preacher, and he did what proved you to be wrong. We can be honest and sincere in boasting about people, and be disappointed in them. Regardless of how much we boast about the greatness of the Lord, we will never be disappointed in him.

Paul boasted about his brethren in Corinth because they promised to give to help poor saints in Judea, but he was not sure they would do what they said they would do. He told them, "Wherefore show ye to them and before the churches, the proof of your love, and of our boasting on your behalf. For as touching the ministering to the saints, it is superfluous for me to write to you: for I know the forwardness of your mind, for which I boast of you to them of Macedonia, that

Achaia was ready a year ago; and your zeal hath provoked very many. Yet have I sent the brethren lest our boasting of you should be in vain in this behalf; that, as I said, ye may be ready: lest haply if they of Macedonia come with me, and find you unprepared, we (that we say not, ye) should be ashamed in this same confident boasting" (2 Corinthians 8:24-9:4).

Just as the brother was ashamed after he had bragged on his mule because of the way the mule acted, so we may be ashamed in our "confident boasting" because of the conduct or failure of one about whom we have boasted.

Dad did buy the mule; the good brother assured him if the mule did not please him he could bring him back and get his money back. Dad took a chance on a money-back **guarantee** mule. He must have felt the mule was at least energetic if he would chase cows, and maybe he thought that mule had "character."

## Stubbornness

Many years ago I heard that a man was driving a mule to his buggy and the mule stopped and refused to go again. The man tried hard to get the mule to start. He coaxed him; he whipped him; and he pleaded with the mule, but the stubborn beast refused to move. A neighbor came along and said, "I know how you can get that mule to move." The man in the buggy said, "Well, tell me." The neighbor said, "Build a fire under him."

The man in the buggy decided to build a fire under the mule. Later he reported on the incident and said, "I built a fire under that mule, and I mean he moved! just far enough to burn up the buggy!

Stubbornness is the disposition of refusing to yield, obey or comply; resisting doggedly; determinded; obstinate. It is a trait which children often display.

Under the law of Moses, if a son was a glutton and a drunkard and was stubborn and rebellious and would not obey his parents after they chastened him, then the parents were commanded to take him out of the city before the elders of the city and declare him to be a glutton and a drunkard and all the men of the city were to stone him to death (Deuteronomy 21:18-21).

Under the gospel system, children are commanded not to be disobedient to their parents. Children that stubbornly disobey their parents are not stoned to death in our society, but such children may bring themselves to an untimely grave through the consequences of their stubbornness!

One of the good reasons the Holy Spirit gave for children obeying their parents was, "That it may be well with thee, and thou mayest live long on the earth" (Ephesians 6:3). If a stubborn son keeps getting drunk even though his parents plead with him to quit, he may get in a car while under the influence of alcohol, and drive at ninety miles an hour and kill himself and others. When such a son or anyone kills himself in that manner, it is not right for a preacher or anyone to say at his funeral, "The Lord saw fit to take him." He saw fit to take himself! If he had lived right, he could have avoided such a horrible death. He could have lived longer on the earth!

Parents are often stubborn too! In fact, a whole generation of people was described by the Holy writer as "a stubborn and rebellious generation that set not their heart aright, and whose spirit was not stedfast with God" (Psalm 78:8). The stubbornness of God's people was so great at one time that Moses cried out to God in their behalf and said to God, "Look not unto the stubbornness of this people, nor to their wickedness, nor to their sin." (Deuteronomy 9:27).

King Saul of Israel disobeyed God and God's prophet, Samuel, told Saul, "Rebellion is as the sin of witchcraft, and stubbornness is iniquity and idolatry" (1 Samuel 15:23). To stubbornly disobey God is just as bad as worshipping idols!

A God-directed writer said of a lewd woman, "She is loud and stubborn; her feet abide not in her house (Proverbs 7:11). The woman who stubbornly refuses to obey God's laws of chastity and purity will lead foolish men to their destruction. Sex is a precious gift of God for two people scripturally married to each other, but people cannot stubbornly ignore God's laws regarding sex without suffering terrible consequences.

The lewd woman of Proverbs 7:11 is described vividly in the rest of that chapter. The man who yields to her flattery is described as, "He goeth after her straightway, as an ox goeth to the slaughter, or as a fool to the correction of the stocks, till a dart strike through his liver; as a bird hasteth to the snare, and knoweth not that it is for his life (Proverbs 7:22, 23).

That mule moved just enough that the buggy was burned up. Perhaps we can learn not only about the ugliness of stubbornness from this mule story, but also the story illustrates the fact that people are sometimes so stubborn that what little they do is destructive instead of helpful!

## Faithful And Dependable

While he was a student at International Bible College, Elihue Thompson told me about his grandfather's courting experiences. When Elihue's grandfather was a young man he traveled several miles in a buggy pulled by a mule to court the girl he married. Often he would go to sleep as he returned home and the mule would take him safely home.

A few times the young man would not wake up when the mule got him home and he would sleep all night in the buggy. The mule would stand quietly and faithfully until morning.

That mule was truly faithful and dependable. He was more faithful and dependable than some people are. He was more faithful and dependable than some members of the church are!

One of the greatest blessings one can have is a friend who is truly faithful and dependable. One of the most disappointing things in one's life is experineced when one he feels is truly his friend proves not to be.

Being really dependable is very important even in little matters! It is good for children to have some jobs around the home even if the jobs are little and seemingly insignificant. They should be expected to do these little jobs if for no other reason than to learn to be dependable.

A member of the church may be faithful in attending all the services of the church and not be really faithful to the Lord. If one who attends all the worship services is not dependable on the job where he works, he is really not faithful to the Lord. "And whatsoever ye do, do it heartily, as to the Lord, and not unto men" (Colossians 3:23).

One should be dependable on his job and work there

as if he were working for Christ. Not being dependable on one's job and not working faithfully for the pay he receives is a species of stealing.

Some members of the church and even some who call themselves gospel preachers do not pay their debts; they evade their financial obligations. It is sad to hear of so many like this. If one is having difficulties meeting his financial obligations, it could be because of poor management. But poor management is poor stewardship. Poor stewardship is a sign of a lack of dependability. One should be careful that he lives within his income. If one's outgo is more than his income, his upkeep will be his downfall!

Sickness or other accidents can cause one to get into financial straits. If you are behind on paying what you owe, do not just ignore your obligations. Go to those you owe and explain your situation. If you can pay just a small amount every week, most of them will be glad to cooperate with you. Do not just evade your obligations; be dependable! Otherwise people will start saying of you, "And he claims to be a Christian." Or if a preacher fails to meet his obligations and to make proper arrangements, people will start saying, "And he claims to be a preacher!"

I read of a man who worked in the woods. One day he told his dog to watch his dinner pail in the woods where he was working. A fire swept through that part of the woods. When the man returned and found his burned dinner pail he also found the charred remains of his dog, and weeping he said, "I should not have told him to stay by that pail because I knew he would do it."

We all should be dependable. How different the world would be if everyone was truly dependable! We cannot conceive of how much more effective the church would be if every member of it was really dependable. So often one in the church is known to say he will do something in the Lord's work but does not do it.

There is no way one can conceive of the grief that has weighed heavily upon human hearts because some were not dependable and did not do what they were supposed to do.

## No Accident

A story is told that a man's mule kicked him and rather severely injured him. A friend said to him. "Don't you imagine your accident policy will cover the medical costs." The mule owner replied, "No, because it was no accident; that mule kicked me on purpose!"

Josh Billings wrote a satire on us humans he called "Essa on the Muel." He said of "Muels" "Tha are like sum men, verry korrupt at harte; ive known them to be good muels for 6 months, just tu git a good chance to kick sumbody."

Josh may have misrepresented mules when he wrote the foregoing. However, it is easy to believe he was right in implying some men would be good six months just to get a chance to swindle or cheat someone.

That mule may have really kicked his master "On purpose," but it is sure that some people do hurtful and damaging deeds to other human beings on purpose!

Solomon said there were some who were so evil they could not sleep unless they had done mischief, and unless they caused some to fall (Proverbs 4:16).

Imagine one's having to take sleeping pills because of his being so mean he could not sleep unless he damaged or hurt or misled someone during the day!

Some of the worst deeds of destruction were not accidents. The most skillful planning and determined deliberation have been behind the most damaging works.

It was no accident that caused the death of Naboth the Jezreelite, but it was the skilled scheming of Queen Jezebel (1 Kings 21).

It is reported that a fellow in North Carolina was put in jail for having married thirteen women. He escaped, and a man recognized him, and being anxious to receive the reward offered for his capture, he asked the polygamist to have dinner at his house. The host slyly slipped out to summon a constable while his wife prepared the meal. Great was his horror when he returned to learn the culprit had run away with his wife!

And that was no accident!

## The Value of Cooperation

The story is told of two mules that were tied to each other, but pulled away from each other. They were near two piles of hay. One wanted to get to one of the piles of provender, and the other was trying to get to the other pile. The two mules finally cooperated and got to eat both piles of hay whereas they could not have eaten either pile had they continued to pull against each other!

It is reported that Henry Ward Beecher expressed admiration for a horse he was riding. The liveryman gleefully replied to preacher Beecher by saying of the horse, "He'll work any place you put him and will do all that any horse can do."

Beecher's confidence in the horse was increased by what the liveryman said, and he said of the horse, "I wish he were a member of my church!"

A lack of cooperation among God's people can be the cause of much grief and woe. In 1 Corinthians chapter 12 the Holy Ghost compared the Lord's church with the human body. God designed the human body so that for it to function properly, its members must cooperate. Even so, members of the body of Christ which is his church, must cooperate for the church to function as it should.

I heard of one brother who placed membership with a congregation. He attended the next business meeting of that church and said to the others there: "Brethren, I want it understood that as long as I attend the business meetings of this church nothing will pass unanimously." What a bad attitude!

A great naturalist, W. H. Hudson reported on a blackbird and a thrush he observed. These two birds frequently met at a bird feeding place. The blackbird would pick up crumbs and put them in the thrush's mouth. The beak of the thrush had been cut off in a trap.

That blackbird was more cooperative and kinder than some people. Too often people take advantage of and abuse other people, even those who may be involved in difficulties.

Even some members of the church have been guilty of abusing others, even other Christians. But, whether a Christian abuses another Christian or a non-Christian, the guilt would be the same!

Such abuse is seen when one may be losing his grip on his job and instead of trying to help him keep his job by encouraging him to do better work, another may work to get it away from him.

Cooperate with those who cannot pick up the crumbs of life like the bird who lost part of his beak: pick them up for them! God made us to live in a world of cooperating with each other.

### We're Acting Like Human Fools!

Two tough old mules said, "Get this dope,
  We're tied together with a piece of rope."
Said one to the other, "You come MY way,
  While I take a nibble of that new-mown hay."
I won't, said the other, You come with ME,
  I have some hay over this way, you see."
So they got nowhere, just pawed up the dirt,
  Pulling each way, how that rope did hurt!
Then faced they about, those stubborn mules,
  And said, "We're acting just like human fools,
Let's pull together, I'll go your way,
  Then you come with me, and we'll both eat hay."
So they ate their hay, and liked it, too.
  And said, "Let's be comrades, good and true."

As the sun went down they were heard to bray,
  "Ah, this is the end of a perfect day."

## *Traces Hang Too Loose*

Maury Deaton told me he lived in a community where a man lived who drove a big horse and a mule to a wagon. (I have ridden many miles in a wagon pulled by a horse and a mule.) The traces of the man's horse were always tight while the traces on the mule were loose.

That horse always pulled his part of the load, plus much of the mule's part, if not all of the mule's part.

That mule was smart in a way, if you say knowing how to keep from working is being smart!

The horse pulled the load; the mule just filled a place! The mule was in the harness, but he still did not do much. His position by the wagon tongue, in the harness, gave him the appearance of doing something, but he did not do much. He might have even hindered the horse at times.

There are people who just fill a place, and do not do much. Some are "In their harness" but they still do not do much. Their "traces hang too loose" too much!

The harness of horses and mules that pulled wagons and buggies in those "good old days" sometimes included holding back straps. These straps were designed so the beasts could hold back the vehicle in some situations.

Some people I have known were "In the harness" but the trouble was that all the harness they seemed to want to wear was the "Holding back straps."

One should not hold back the Lord's work. One should not just fill a place and let his "traces hang loose." He should do his part wherever he is situated!

One man on a job was asked by a visitor: "How long have you been working here?" He replied, "Ever since the boss threatened to fire me." One should do his part where he works.

Every student in a shcool should do his part to make the school what it ought to be. There is no excuse for laziness, and yet laziness causes much grief and disturbance in schools, in homes, and in the church.

Boast not of your acumen and skill
　Nor tell how you're so smart
Unless you exercise your will
　And do your best to take your part!
There's no substitute for work
　Its the way to get your start'
Your tasks never, never shirk
　But always take your part.

# A Mule Watchtower!

An Alabamian told me about how some boys used to do their father. Their father would leave his boys to work in a field, but they usually did not do as much work as they should have done.

When the boys wanted to "goof off" and play, one of them would stand on the back of one of their mules so he could see over a ridge and watch for the father. When he could see the father coming he would tell the rest of the boys and they would all go to work!

The mule was used as a "watch tower" and could not be blamed for such trickery and deceit, but the boys displayed a species of disobedience. Any father would expect his sons to have some fun and to play and rest some, but evidently in this case the boys knew they were overdoing such and not working enough.

Having been a boy that grew up on farms under the guidance of a father who seemed to always be able to find plenty of work for us to do, I understand how those boys wanted to get out of work. The genius and schemes of young boys to get out of work is one of the truly astounding phenomenon of human experience!

Young boys are not the only ones who scheme to get out of work. I have known some young men who said they wanted to become preachers of the gospel and who were supported financially in school where they were supposed to get some training toward becoming preachers, but would not do their work in school in studying their courses as they should.

I believe a young man is stealing who takes money from brethren so he can go to school to be trained to become a gospel preacher but will not do the work in school that he should do.

Hiding from the boss and not working properly on a

job in industry is a form of stealing. An employee should do an honest day's work for a day's pay whether his boss is watching or not! "Servants, obey in all things your masters according to the flesh, not with eyeservice, as menpleasers; but in singleness of heart, fearing God: and whatsoever ye do, do it heartily, as to the Lord, and not unto men; knowing that of the Lord ye shall receive the reward of the inheritance: for ye serve the Lord Christ. But he that doeth wrong shall receive for the wrong done and there is no respect of persons. Masters, give unto your servants that which is just and equal; knowing that ye also have a Master in heaven" (Colossians 3:22-25; 4:1).

The foregoing scripture was written to regulate the Master and slave relationships that existed when Paul lived. There is no direct command in this passage or any other passage in the New Testament that enjoined the immediate dissolution of such a relationship, but the principles taught in such passages, if followed, were designed to do away with slavery.

The same principles if followed in the employer and employee relationship of our own time will so regulate the relationship so that both employers and employees will be treated equitably and justly.

Christian employees should not work merely as menpleasers with "eyeservice," which means do not do your work just to please your employer, but do your work "Heartily, as to the Lord, and not unto men." "Heartily" of the text is from Greek *ek psuches* which means out of the soul! Christians should do their work well on the job "fearing God." A Christian's respect for the awesomeness of Almighty God should cause him to be a good worker on his job.

Too many, it appears, work just to get a pay check. It is right to get a pay check, and it should be a proper pay check for work performed, but one should be a good worker because he is working as if he were working for the Lord.

If all employers and employees were Christians and truly followed the principles taught in the New Testament there would be no trouble between them!

Whether you stand on a mule to get out of work, or if you in some other way try to avoid doing as you should, you are wrong!

## Fred Humiliated Five Cowboys

In 1979 the church of Christ in Brilliamt, Alabama had me deliver a series of lectures there on the Bible versus Evolution. I presented two of the lectures in the Brilliant High School Gymnasium.

While in Brilliant I took a walk. While walking I saw a gentleman standing in his yard looking across the beautiful valley near his house. When I saw him I thought of an old friend in Overton County, Tennessee named Stanley Carr, because the form and features of the gentleman reminded me of Stanley.

I asked the gentleman if I could go to an old cemetery I could see back of his house about a hundred yards. He said, "Yes, you may." I said, "What is your name." He said, "Edgar Carr." I was astonished, I told him that when I first saw him I thought of Stanley Carr of Overton County, Tennessee. He said, "All of us Carrs are kin."

As Edgar and I talked more I soon learned he was a Christian. We walked to the cemetery and looked it over. He told me he had had five mules on his place, but that the last one he had died October 29, 1979 which was less than two weeks before. That mule's name was Fred.

Edgar told me he owned Fred about nine years, and that the mule was about nine years of age when he got him from Coy Guin who lives on Pea Ridge in Marion County, Alabama.

Brother Carr told me that no one was ever able to ride Fred and stay on him. He said while Coy owned him five cowboys were in a rodeo at Hackleburg, Alabama and rode mules in it. Coy told the cowboys he had a mule no one had ever ridden and stayed on him. The confident cowboys told Coy to bring the mule to the rodeo and they said "We will ride him or tell you why!"

Coy took Fred to the rodeo and all five of the skilled cowboys tried to ride him, but he threw every one of them. They could not ride Fred!

The foregoing is a case of a mule humiliating confident men.

It is good to be confident, but it is dangerous to be over-confident.

I well recall a shipmate in the U.S. Navy who told me he knew how to get around in New York City. As we approached that great metropolis on a train in 1946, he told me repeatedly to stay with him as we went sight seeing in New York. He was very confident about his knowledge of the city. Being from the country, and being on my way to Millington, Tennessee where I was to be discharged from the Navy, I surely did not want to get lost in the big city!

My friend and I walked from Grand Central Station and had an exciting and very interesting tour. But had I followed his guidance we would not have got back to the train on time. I had to tell him the way back to the station!

The Lord's apostles were over confident about their loyalty to Jesus. The Lord told his apostles, "All ye shall be offended because of me this night..." Peter responded by saying, "Though all men shall be offended because of thee, yet will I never be offended." Then Jesus told Peter, "Verily I say unto thee, that this night, before the cock crow, thou shalt deny me thrice. Peter then said unto him, "Though I should die with thee, yet will I not deny thee. Likewise also said all the disciples" (Matthew 26:31-35).

Peter did just as Jesus said he would do, and all the other apostles forsook Jesus and fled when the going got rough! (Matthew 26:56; 69-75)

There is only one thing that accounts for the fact that after the apostles forsook Jesus and fled, they were loyal to him in the preaching of the gospel. That one thing is the resurrection of Jesus! (1 Peter 1:3)

## He Was Afraid Of Something New!

Seth Cozart told me that his Dad, H. D. Cozart was driving his team of mules to a wagon in Carroll County near McKenzie many years ago. The team was accustomed to going over a bridge that was fifty-five feet long. A new plank had been put in the bridge and one of H. D.'s mules stopped when he saw that new plank, and of course thereby forced the other mule to stop. The other mule was perfectly willing to proceed and do what he was supposed to do, but his team-mate held him back!

The fearful mule not only would not proceed over the bridge, Seth said he backed the wagon into the ditch which was about ten feet deep!

How typical of us humans! Even in the church one person can, and often does, hold others back and keeps them from proceeding as they should in the Lord's work!

That trifling mule was afraid of a new plank! That mule had no reason to be afraid. But sometimes mules, like people, are not reasonable. The new plank was even better than the old plank! The new was better than what the mule was used to.

Some things may not be as good as the old things they replace. Some new things may really be bad. But, a thing is not bad just because it is new to us!

Learn to adjust to the new things that are good, and to those that are even better than the things they replace, and go right on and do what God wants you to do in obedience to his will even when you find a new and better method of doing it.

For an example, if you have been doing personal evangelism, and you find a better method than you have been using, do not refuse to use it just because it is new. By all means, even if you do not want to use the new method, do not keep others from using it. Don't back the wagon into the creek!

## A Mule Died For Them!

Many years ago at Deanfield in Ohio County, Ky., Harold Bellamy heard two elderly men who had worked in coal mines tell about their being trapped in a mine following a cave-in.

The men said they were using carbide lamps, and they were working a mule in the mine. They said the mule got terribly excited and was breathing deeply and rapidly.

The space where the men and the mule were trapped was very small. The men realized that their air supply was very limited. They also realized that the mule was using much more of the air than they were, so they decided they should kill the mule.

One of the men had a hawk bull knife with which he cut the mule's jugular vein. The two men said the mule did not even flinch but stood still and bowed his head and seemed to sense he was to die. They said it was a pitiful sight in the light of their carbide lights. The mule bled to death!

When the men were finally found, so little air remained where they were trapped that they were very weak and about to become unconcious. No doubt they would have died had they not killed the mule! That mule died for them!

I am confident every reader of the foregoing story will be emotionally stirred and moved by it. What a sad scene indeed! A faithful mule bleeding to death!

I wonder if the same readers are as emotionally stirred when they read the story of Jesus and his bleeding to death to save all men from eternal death! If we are not careful we will become indifferent and careless when we hear the story of Calvary and not be moved by that awful ordeal of our Saviour's dying for us. God forbid that we should become so careless and cold about the crucifixion of Christ!

In a sermon I intend to tell the story of the mule who died for two men. I am afraid my doing so will arouse more emotions for the mule than my telling about Jesus dying for all men.I can visualize even sleepy people in the audience becoming wide awake and more emotionally moved as I tell the sad story of the dying mule than some are moved when I tell the story of my dying Saviour!

A preacher was telling about Jesus dying on Calvary. Very eloquently and with great pathos he told how Jesus suffered for our sins. A little girl was sitting among adults that were showing little or no emotion as the preacher described the agony on Golgotha. The little girl was being greatly moved by the story of how the soldiers nailed the Lord to the Roman cross, and how finally one of Caesar's servants pierced the side of Jesus with a spear. The little girl's emotions peaked with an outburst from her sweet innocent lips and she exclaimed with the full force of her voice, "Oh, why did they do it?"

That precious little girl's heart was so tender and it was easily touched with the story of the cross. But many around her had become calloused and hardened and were not moved by the massage that saves dying souls.

Beloved, let us be very careful lest we be more moved by the story of a dying mule, than by the story of our dying Saviour!

# Species and Kind

"And these are the children of Zibean; both Ajah, and Anah: this was that Anah that found the mules in the wilderness, as he fed the asses of Zibeon his father" (Genesis 36:24).

In Genesis 36, Moses recorded "the generations of Esau who is Edom." For some reason he mentioned that one of Esau's descendants, Anah, found the mules in the wilderness, as he fed his father's asses. Evidently this finding of the mules made Anah distinctive. Could it be that the people had not known before that when a male ass (donkey) and a female horse are mated, their off-spring is a mule? Was this the reason Anah's discovery of the mules was worthy of the attention of an inspired writer? Or was it because he found such a large number of mules? We cannot know for sure.

There is one thing we can know, and that is that mules are an example of variation in a *kind*. Moses mentioned at least ten times in the first chapter of Genesis that there were *kinds* of plants and animals from the very beginning. One cannot believe this and also believe theistic evolution which says there was just a blob of life in the beginning and from that over millions of years there finally developed the kinds.

Men have made tables to classify plants and animals. The tables are known as *tables of taxonomy*. Taxonomy is from the Greek infinitive *tassein* which means to classify or to arrange. Man's arrangement of living things includes what he calls species. *Species* does not necessarily mean the same as what kind *means* in Genesis. There are variations in a kind. Some may say the Bible is not reliable because it teaches that each kind produces after its kind. They may insist that the horse and the donkey being two species and mating and having an off-spring known as a mule is proof that the Bible is inaccurate in what it says about each bringing forth after its kind. But this is a false conclusion, because *kind* is a broader category than species.

God could have made kinds in the beginning with variations in them. For example he could have made horses and donkeys within a kind on the day he created animals. Or, he may have created the horse kind of animals with a genetical potential in them so that the variations could develop within the kind. Think of all the variations in mankind. Since there has been off-spring of a donkey and a zebra called a zeonkey, it is obvious that the zebra is also in the same kind as the horse, donkey and mule. One might object that there is too much difference in appearance of a donkey and a zebra for them to be in the same kind. But that is not a valid argument because the variations in appearance of those of us in mankind are as great or greater than the variations in appearance of those in horsekind.

What Anah discovered in the wilderness was proof that donkeys had been mating horses, because horses and donkeys are of the same kind.

The mule rarely ever has off-spring. There have been a few cases where mules had off-spring. But the off-spring of a mule is not an example for evolutionists because the off-spring of a mule is a reversion in kind to its ancestors instead of being less like its ancestors. The mule virtually says, "This thing has gone far enough."

76

## Answering Folly

It is reported that a preacher called the Health Department and said he had found a dead mule on his property and that he felt the Department would want to get the carcass and dispose of it. A "smart alec" answered the phone at the Department. He said to the preacher, "You're a preacher ain't ya? don't you bury the dead?"

The preacher replied, "Yes, I'm a preacher, and I help bury the dead, but I always try to notify the next of kin first."

Solomon wrote: "Answer not a fool according to his folly, lest thou also be like unto him. Answer a fool according to his folly, lest he be wise in his own conceit." (Proverbs 26:4,5)

The foregoing seems to be contradictory, but it is not. You should not answer a fool in a manner so that your answer makes you appear to be as big a fool as he is. However, you should answer a fool in a manner so that he will not feel he is wise in his own conceit.

Martha Ostenso said that conceit is a little country bounded on the north, south, east, and west by yourself. Conceit is also defined as "a personal quality that makes an ignoramus satisfied with himself."

*Folly* in Proverbs 26:5,6 is from the Hebrew word *iv-veleth* and is defined as *silliness.*

One should not answer a fool's silliness so that his answer makes him appear to be as silly as the fool he is answering. But one should answer a fool's silliness in a manner that will expose the silliness of the one he is answering so that the one he is answering will not think he is wise in his own conceit.

A fool may think he has said something worth hearing, or he may think he has put another to silence. In such a case he should be answered so that he will know he has not really displayed superior intelligence and so he will not be wise in his own conceit.

I read about a tourist who drove into a small town and stopped to get gasoline. He asked an old man at the station, "How long has this place been dead?" The old man replied: "Not long; you are the first buzzard to get here." Did he answer the tourist properly?

## He Took His Boss Seriously

My wife Margie and I have many dear friends, and none are dearer than Huford and Bertha Mathis of Lawrenceburg, Tennessee.

Bertha told me of an interesting incident in the life of her father. I knew her father, brother A.P. Rigsby; he was a mighty good man. He worked for another mighty good man that I knew, brother J.H. Stribbling. Brother Stribbling was a good Christian business man. I will never forget that in 1948 when I was a young preacher he gave me twenty dollars to give my wife. That was quite a sum of money to us in 1948.

Many years ago, brother Rigsby was supervisor over a log hauling project in which brother Stribbling was engaged. Brother Rigsby had great difficulty with one of the mules that was being worked in pulling a log wagon. He had great difficulty getting a bridle on the mule and getting him harnessed for the task. He even tried getting in a loft and letting a sack down over the mule's face so he could not see one who approached with a bridle. That mule must have had character!

Finally brother Rigsby told brother Stribbling about how difficult it was to harness the mule, and asked what he should do. Brother Stribbling lightly replied, "Just knock him in the head." Brother Rigsby did just that; he hit the mule so hard he killed him. Before being too critical of the action of this good brother, I suggest you try harnessing such a mule a few times.

Anyway, perhaps brother Stribbling did not mean for brother Rigsby to take what he told him so seriously.

I suppose this story should teach us to be careful what we tell others; they might take us seriously!

There is a time and place for levity and light talk as

long as it is not harmful, and as long as it is obviously not serious. But most of our words should be of such nature that they can be taken seriously.

Jesus said, "And I say unto you, that every idle word that men shall speak, they shall give account thereof in the day of judgment" (Matthew 12:36). Apparently some misunderstand the word *idle* in the foregoing text and think that one should never use any light words or words of levity. However, *idle* in the text is from the Greek word *argon* and one of the meanings is *injurious*. This is its obvious meaning in Matthew 12:36 because of the contextual setting in which it is used.

## He Went Back Home

It was my pleasure to speak in a series of meetings at Union Hill congregation near Hardin, Ky.

While at Union Hill, one of the Christians there, Leonas Smith told me a mule story. He said his great-grandmother's brother, Jarett Haymes, drove a team of mules to a wagon from Marshall County, Kentucky (where Union Hill church is located) to a place in Texas. After getting settled in Texas, one of the mules got out of the enclosure where Jarett had put the mules and that mule went back to Marshall County Kentucky. This happened long ago before bridges were built over the Mississippi River, so brother Smith said.

That mule must have wanted to go back to his native land very much. God made mules and other animals with remarkable instinctive powers. Animals do many things which they do not have to learn to do, or train to do. God made them so they could do such.

There is a species of birds known as Manx sherwater. Some of these live in burrows in the cliffs of Wales overlooking the great Atlantic Ocean. One of these was taken from his home in the cliffs of an island near Wales and carried to Boston, Mass. On June 4, 1952, he was tagged and turned loose in Boston. Twelve days later, on June 16 at 1:30 p.m. that bird crawled into his home on the cliffs near Wales, after a 3,050 mile flight across the mighty Atlantic!

In a recent issue of Grit Magazine there was the story of Blackie. Garrell Horn of O'Fallon, Illinois took his family on a camping trip to Eldon, Missouri in August 1973. The Horns took Blackie their cat with them. Blackie got lost and for five days Garrell looked for Blackie in the streets and alleys in Eldon, also he searched for Blackie over the rural areas around Eldon.

Mr. Horn offered rewards for Blackie through newspaper and radio announcements. But, Blackie was not found. Finally, the Horns went back home to O'Fallon, Illinois which is a 200 mile trip.

On November 6 a neighbor called the Horns and said a black cat was at their house. Dr. Orville Minton a veterinarian that had performed two operations on Blackie confirmed that the cat was the Horn's cat named Blackie.

Mr. Horn said, "Judging from the creosote on her paws we think she might have followed the railroad tracks through Missouri and across the Missouri and Mississippi Rivers." Blackie's footpads were worn down considerably.

There is only one way to account for the fantastic feats of animals, birds, etc., and that is by saying that God made them so they could do such wonderful things.

Jarett Haymes' mule did better than some members of the Lord's church. When some members of the church get away from "home" (the church) and go back into the world, they never find their way back "home." But, they could get back if they wanted to. They may not get back without help. Each Christian who is faithful should feel keenly his responsibility to help straying brothers and sisters get back "home."

"Brethren, if any of you do err from the truth, and one convert him; let him know that he which converteth the sinner from the error of his way shall save a soul from death, and shall hide a multitude of sins" (James 5:19,20). This text tells us: (1) Even an erring brother can be classed as a sinner. (2) Not just preachers and elders are responsible for trying to convert an erring brother, but the passage is addressed to brethren! (3) The erring brother (or sinner) *is a soul!* Note: "Shall save a soul." (4) Getting an erring brother to come back to the Lord is saving a soul from death. The *death* of the text is not physical death but separation from God, because faithful children of God do not escape physical death.

I would admonish all erring brethren to do as well as Jarett Haymes' mule did. Come back home!

## Vengeance

I suppose no one really understands or appreciates some of the manners of mules. Despite all the good mules have done, they have always done some things that seemed so unnecessary. They are that much like people.

A sample of bad mule manners is seen in the report that came to me about a mule that switched his tail into the face of his master on a cold morning.

When it is cold there seems to be so little reason for a mule to switch his tail, because flies would not be bothering him on a cold morning. But mules, like humans, do some things for what seems to be no good reason.

That mule that switched his tail so harshly into his master's face had a bountiful supply of cockleburs in his tail which made the whole ordeal seem even more unreasonable, and a lot more painful to the mule's owner! It may be that the mule enjoyed the act more because of the cockleburs!

Naturally, the mule's owner did not like the cockleburs crashing into his face. He tried to get vengeance on the mule by striking one of the mule's hip bones with his bare hand very hard. Of course, this was felt very little by the mule. But the man broke a knuckle bone and when the story came to me, the man was reported to still be bothered with a clumsy knuckle-bone that showed signs of having been broken!

In an act of vengeance it is hard to get even with a mule.

Napoleon said vengenance has no foresight. Obviously, in most cases foresight would prevent vengeance.

Some of the worst deeds of history were those done by men who were taking vengeance on their offenders. Man's vengeance merely makes bad matters worse.

We cannot adequately conceive of how different history would have been had all recognized and lived by the following admonition, "Dearly, beloved, avenge not yourselves, but rather give place unto wrath, for it is written, Vengeance is mine; I will repay saith the Lord. Therefore, if thine enemy hunger, feed him; if he thirst, give him drink: for in so doing thou shalt heap coals of fire on his head. Be not overcome with evil, but overcome evil with good" (Romans 12:19-21).

I knew a preacher of whom it was told that a man cursed him severely. It is reported that the preacher just looked at the man and held his eyes on him until the one who had cursed him began to weep. He heaped coals of fire on his head!

One woman misunderstood the figurative meaning of heaping coals of fire on a person's head. It is reported that she was telling a preacher how she had tried about everything on her husband to get him to do right. The preacher asked her, "Have you tried heaping coals of fire on his head?" Whereupon the woman replied, "No, but I tried hot scalding coffee!"

There is a vengeance foretold which might help keep you from taking vengeance if you think about it. This vengeance was announced by Paul when he said the Lord Jesus shall be revealed "in flaming fire taking vengeance on them that know not God, and that obey not the gospel of our Lord Jesus Christ" (2 Thessalonians 1:7,8).

# Propriety

Will Totty told me several years ago about a pet mule he had when he was a boy in Hickman County Tennessee. He said the mule followed him wherever he would let him.

The Tottys lived in a house with a front door that was an entrance directly out of the front yard into the living room. One day little Will decided to see what his pet mule would do if he walked close by the front of the house when the front door was open. As he started the mule followed him until he came to that open door. That open door was more than the mule could resist. He paused and looked into the living room, and then went into that room, and in typical mule style he wallowed on the living room floor.

Many readers perhaps do not know what a mule does when he wallows. He lays down and turns his body from one side to the other several times.

Will said when his pet got through wallowing and came back into the yard; the living room was considerably changed and the furniture was damaged.

No one in his right mind would think of forbidding a mule to engage in wallowing on the ground, for even in the mud a mule seems to greatly relish the act. It seems the dirtier he gets, the better he likes it. However, everything should be done in its proper place. A living room is not the place for a mule to wallow. It seems that even a mule would sense the impropriety of such.

Unfortunately, some of us humans seem not to sense the lack of propriety in some things we do.

There is nothing wrong with chewing gum. But it seems out of place to chew gum when in the assembly of the saints for worship. It seems many have decided this after getting inside the church building. If you need evidence of this, take a look underneath the average pew! The average church building that has been standing as long as fifteen or twenty years probably contains a gallon of gum.

Can you imagine what a huge hill all this pew putty would make if all of it under all the pews of America were collected and heaped into one pile?

There is nothing wrong with discussing surgery, how painful it is, etc. However to introduce this subject in a hospital and to discuss it with one who is about to have surgery is in poor taste.

To talk with one who has had surgery or who is about to have surgery and to tell him you had a friend or friends who died following surgery is more out of place than a mule's wallowing in a living room!

## Going From One Danger To Another

When I was a boy someone told me about a mule that started across a bridge. There was a hole near one side of the bridge. The mule was so afraid of that hole that in his attempts to go by it at a safe distance he went off the bridge on the other side!

It was proper that that mule be cautious about that hole in the bridge. But, he should not have been so unduly cautious that he was careless about another hazard that was even more dangerous to him than the hole.

A common error committed by us human beings is the error of being so cautious and alarmed about some dangers that we are unaware of other matters that are equally dangerous, or even more dangerous than that which alarms us.

The course of humans is often the course of going from one extreme to the other. Long before Jesus was born people plagued themselves with this plight. This was the problem Aristotole dealt with in his practical philosophy concerning the "golden mean," or the happy medium.

A black preacher brother came to me several years ago in Kentucky and talked with me about the negative doctrine and attitude known as anti-ism. This doctrine had almost destroyed a congregaton where he was preaching in a series of meetings. The congregation was finally completely destroyed by this doctrine.

The black brethren are better at summing up situations than the rest of us. The black preacher who came to me said concerning the folks who were espousing anti-ism, "Some brethren are so afraid they will do wrong, they won't do right."

There is the danger of going into a position that is

liberal and unscriptural as we attempt to get away from the unduly negative position of anti-ism. So Christians need to be cautious and pursue the course that is scriptural.

There is also the danger of falling into the sin of failing to do what the Lord wants us to do in the work of evangelism.

It is right and proper to fight error, whether it is anti-ism or liberalism. But if that is all we do, we will fail to tell the world the story of the cross and God's plan of salvation for the lost.

Albert Hill said if he goes fishing he might have to kill some snakes, but he would not want to spend all his time killing snakes; he would want to do some fishing too!

It is right to be afraid of error, but one of the greatest errors one can commit is the error of failing to do what God commands you to do all because you were concerned about another kind of error.

One could spend his whole life fighting error and still die and go to torment if he failed to do other things God told him to do.

"Therefore to him that knoweth to do good, and doeth it not, to him it is sin" (James 4:17).

Do not make the mistake that mule made. In going by "a hole in a bridge" at a cautious distance, be careful that you do not go off the bridge on the other side into the ditch and danger of not doing what you should do!

## Avoiding Work

Charles Coil told me about a plantation owner in Arkansas who had eighty mules. One of his mules was ocassionally hard to find. On one ocassion some workmen looked for a long time before they found the clever beast. They found him hiding in the water of a drainage ditch. They suspected the mule hid to get out of work.

It seems that many people make considerable effort to keep from working. Some are not afraid of work; they go to sleep right beside it!

It is reported that one man said he could not stand to see his wife work, so when she was working he would always go into another room!

A specific reason for withdrawing from a brother was stated by Paul when he wrote, "If a man will not work neither should he eat" (2 Thessalonians 3:6-11).

Paul said that working not at all was walking disorderly, and that some were not working at all but were busybodies. How could one be a busybody but not work at all? The Greek word in Paul's statement is defined: "to do a thing with excessive or superflous care; to be a busy body."

Evidently Paul meant some were very busy in other people's business but not doing anything about their own business.

Paul referred to some who were idle, but who were tattlers and busybodies speaking what they should not speak (1 Timothy 5:13). Verily if the elbows and knuckles of some were as exercised as their jawbones they could greatly improve the world!

Do not be like the Arkansas mule and hide to get out of work.

Don Herold said that work is the greatest thing in

the world and that we should always save some of it for tomorrow.

Walter Courtenay said, "God gave man work, not to burden him, but to bless him, and useful work, willingly, cheerfully, effectively done, has always been the finest expression of the human spirit."

Winston Churchill said workers are soldiers with different weapons but the same courage.

God's Word says, "Go to the ant, thou sluggard; consider her ways, and be wise: which having no guide, overseer, or ruler, provideth her meat in the summer, and gathereth her food in the harvest. How long wilt thou sleep, O sluggard? When wilt thou arise out of thy sleep? Yet a little sleep, a little slumber, a little folding of the hands to sleep: so shall thy poverty come as one that travelleth, and thy want as an armed man" (Proverbs 6:6-11).

It is all right to dream, but do not oversleep: if you do your dreams will never come true.

It is doubtful that work has killed as many as idleness has killed! Someone said, "Idleness is the sepulchre of a living man."

## Just Trying To Be Helpful

My brother, Gene Overton of Bowling Green, Kentucky told me about visiting with a Kentucky couple. The wife told Gene she saw a mule do a very unusual deed.

The Kentucky woman told Gene that a cow had left her new calf, perhaps to go for water, and a mule took the calf in his mouth and started toward the barn with it. The mule took a portion of the calf's loose skin between his teeth and the calf thus hanged from the mule's mouth as the mule took it to the barn.

The mule let the calf back to the ground and then picked it up again, and repeated this action several times before reaching the barn.

Some men tried to get the calf from the mule but the mule violently reacted and would not allow them to do so. The men thought the mule was going to harm the calf or perhaps kill it.

Evidently the mule thought the men were trying to harm the calf. He would not let the men near the calf until he got the calf to the barn. That Kentucky mule was just trying to be helpful, but the calf really did not need the care the mule gave to it.

Often people try to be helpful when no help is needed, and in some cases the consequences are no more harmful than in the case of the mule carrying the calf to the barn. But, in other cases the consequences may be grievous.

Sarai was trying to be helpful when she said to Abram, "Behold now, the Lord hath restrained me from bearing; I pray thee, go in unto my maid; it may be that I may obtain children by her. And Abram hearkened to the voice of Sarai" (Genesis 16:2).

As a result of Sarai's trying to be helpful, her maid,

Hagar, had a son by Abram who was named Ishmael.

Later God fulfilled his promise to Abram (or Abraham) and caused Sarai (or Sarah) to have a son who was named Isaac. There was strife between Ishmael and Isaac. Their descendents have had much strife. The conflict in the Middle East is a conflict between the descendents of Ishmael and Isaac. It was all started by Sarai trying to be helpful when no help was needed! Perhaps Sarai constituted the first "Ladies' Aid Society."

When you try to be helpful, do better than the Kentucky mule and help where help is really needed.

ROMEO AND JULIET

93

## Knowledge Makes A Big Difference

Carson Burroughs told me a story about two men digging a well. They reached a depth that required that one of them stay in the well loading a bucket with dirt while the other one stayed on the ground surface pulling the loaded bucket with a rope to the surface.

When the man in the well was getting quite deep in the good earth, the man on the surface told him he was going after some water they could drink. There was a blind mule in the lot where the well was being dug. The mule wore a bell on his neck. The man who went after the water thought it would be funny to pull a little prank on his co-worker in the well.

The man who went after the water took the bell off the mule and walked toward the well, stamping his feet and ringing the bell as he went. He walked around the well and the man in the well became frightened. He thought of the possibility that that blind mule would fall into the well on top of him. He was horrified! He began to yell to the mule. He would cry out, "Gee," then "Haw." (These terms mean "go right," and "go left" in talking to a mule.) Then he would pray; then yell "Gee," and "Haw" again, etc.

Finally the man with the bell went back to the mule and put the bell back on him, and then went and got the water. When he got to the well he started to let the container of water down in the bucket to his partner in the well. His partner yelled at him and said, "I don't want any water, I want to get out of here; I have had an awful experience. That blind mule almost fell in on me!"

That prank was funny in a sense, but really it was too hard on the man in the well to really be amusing to him. Maybe it was, after he thought about it awhile.

This story does illustrate how we can be deceived into thinking there is danger when there really is no danger. It also illustrates what a difference knowledge can make! Had the man in the well known what was really happening he could have turned the joke on his partner and ignored the prank!

Knowledge does make such a big difference! I have often thought of the grief my maternal grandparents must have endured near the close of the nineteenth century because their first four children died with diptheria; two of them within a week. That was before medical men knew what to do to fight diptheria. What a difference such knowledge would have made to my grandparents and thousands of others who suffered similar losses during that era.

"Knowledge is power." President Madison is quoted as having said, "If a people expects to be free and ignorant at the same time, they expect that which cannot be." If we lose our freedom it will be because of ignorance.

It is said that in the last seventy-five years the United States has given a high-school education to more people than all the rest of the world has. This means that seven per cent of the world's population has exceeded ninety-three per cent of the world in this type of educational endeavor. However, with all this educating the United States has more crime than ever. This has to mean that many people in our land are still ignorant of what they really need to know.

The only way we can stop crime is by teaching people the gospel. Those who are ignorant of the great moral principles of the gospel are dangerous! (Read 1 Timothy 1:9-11)

Jesus said, "Ye shall know the truth, and the truth shall make you free" (John 8:32). Our Lord referred primarily to being made free from sin in that text. Some learn much but remain in sin, because they do not learn the truth. (2 Timothy 3:7)

Yes, indeed, knowledge makes a big difference! Fellow Christians I urge you to learn more of God's word and teach God's truth to others at every opportunity. This is the most urgent matter of all.

I urge those who are not Christians to seek to know God's truth. Your knowing and obeying God's truth will completely change your life for the better! Try it and see!

## A Severe Prank

In 1939 my parents moved from one farm to another a distance of eight miles. I well recall my Dad letting me drive old "Rusty" to the buggy that eight miles. Perhaps many of my readers have never even seen a buggy.

I heard about one preacher who got a buggy ride. A man driving a mule to a buggy asked the preacher to go home with him for dinner. The preacher was delighted.

After a rather long haul by the mule, the man driving turned the mule and buggy into the yard of a house. He told the preacher to get out and wait on the porch until he got his mule unharnessed and fed.

Instead of taking care of his mule he drove the mule to where he really lived. The preacher waited on the porch for a long time and began to realize he was the victim of a prank. He discovered no one lived in the house where he was waiting.

That was a rather severe prank to play on a hungry preacher. The preacher was rather severely deceived. But, he suffered no really bad consequences from the prank.

Some preachers have been proven to be deceivers. The Bible warns of such. "But evil men and seducers shall wax worse and worse, deceiving and being deceived" (2 Timothy 3:13). "Now I beseech you, brethren, mark them which cause divisions and offenses contrary to the doctrine which ye have learned; and avoid them. For they that are such serve not our Lord Jesus Christ, but their own belly; and by good words and fair speeches deceive the hearts of the simple" (Romans 16:17,18).

Some people try to indict the Bible by saying it is the

cause of religious divisions. Some even say, "You can prove anything by the Bible." This is libel on the Bible! One can prove only the truth by the Bible! The Bible is not a textbook that contains the contradictory and conflicting doctrines of error that cause religious division. The Bible is the word of God, and God is not the author of confusion, but of peace (1 Corinthians 14:33).

The Bible is the only book that can unite people in religion.

Preachers who deceive people with doctrines that are contrary to what the Bible teaches are the cause of most religious divisions.

Jesus said to his apostles, "Go ye into all the world, and preach the gospel to every creature. He that believeth and is baptized shall be saved; but he that believeth not shall be damned" (Mark 16:15,16). This message will unite people in Christ. People are divided by the deceptive doctrine that says, "He that believeth and is *not* baptized shall be saved."

It would be somewhat humiliating to be deceived by a prankster who was driving a mule to a buggy. But, such would be nothing compared to being deceived by a doctine that would lead you to eternal torment.

## Breaking Habits

In April of 1975 it was my pleasure to preach in another series of gospel meetings with the Lord's people in Henderson, Tennessee. One of the highlights of the week was being with brother and sister E.D. Brigance, who have passed on to be with Jesus. His brother L.L. Brigance was one of my favorite teachers and a true friend.

While I was in Henderson brother Brigance told me about a man who had a mule which he worked at a mill. The mule was required to walk in a circle day after day for many years.

Finally, the man retired the mule and turned him out to graze and rest. But the mule's master was surprised to observe that the mule did not rest; he saw the mule out in the pasture walking in a circle. He was so used to walking in a circle that he continued to do so even when he was retired.

This mule story illustrates how difficult it is for humans to break habits. Some habits are all right, but some are signs of poor judgment; and some are sinful.

Each of us should search his life and see what habits he has which he really should eliminate. A person should have enough will power to stop a bad habit. But all recognize it is not easy to break a habit. Horace Mann said that a habit is a cable which one weaves; a thread of it every day, and at last he cannot break it."

There is a Czech proverb that says, "A habit is a shirt made of iron."

Habits in a sense are the building blocks of character. Good habits are a sign of good character. An icicle is formed by water's freezing a drop at the time. Clear water can form an icicle that sparkles in sunlight like a diamond. If water that forms an icicle is muddy the icicle is not a specimen of beauty. Even so a life, a character, is not beautiful if it is formed by one's adding bad habits, gradually, one at the time, to his life.

If each thought, and habit of one's life is pure, bright, and lovely his life sparkles like a diamond in sunlight.

It is reported that General Sheridan was involved in a battle near a corral where a large number of old, weary war-horses were kept. During the heavy firing they grew warlike and charged upon a number of mules and killed some of them. They also overthrew a rail fence and kept up wild demonstrations until the firing of the battle ceased.

Habits in man and brute are powerful. We are all creatures of habit.

"Finally, brethren, whatsoever things are honest, whatsoever things are just; whatsoever things are pure, whatsoever things are lovely, whatsoever things are of good report; if there be any virtue, and if there by any praise, think on these things" (Philippians 4:8).

Do not excuse yourself and continue in bad habits by saying "I can't help it." Toyohiko Kagawa reports that one of the most used expressions in Japan is, "shikatago nai," which means, "It can't be helped."

We should be people who cry out concerning a bad habit, "It can be helped."

Ferri of Italy, said concerning the psychology of women criminals that those who became criminals after age 27 had little hope of reformation.

Beware of bad habits! The way to break them is to drop them! Tell yourself you can drop them! Do not say "I can't help it."

# A Mother-in-law and a Mule

While I visited in his home more than thirty years ago, Will Ethridge, a gospel preacher told me a story. Will had a good sense of humor. He went on to his eternal reward several years ago.

Brother Ethridge told me about a man who saw a crowd of people gathered at a neighbor's house named Joe. He inquired of another neighbor as to what caused the crowd to gather. The neighbor said, "Joe's mule kicked his mother-in-law and killed her." The man said, "Oh, the crowd has gathered to express sympathy." The neighbor said, "No, they are trying to buy Joe's mule."

Probably brother Ethridge knew this story was just a joke, but there was some reason for it to be told the first time.

No doubt mothers-in-law, generally, are wonderful women, but it is sadly true that some of them have earned the wrong kind of reputation. This no doubt is why so many jokes have been made about mothers-in-law.

I heard about one man whose mother-in-law had driven his new Cadillac over a high cliff. It is reported he had mixed emotions!

I am confident there are many husbands who can truthfully say their mothers-in-law are a great blessing in their lives. My mother-in-law, Mrs. Una Medling was a mighty good Christian woman. She passed to her eternal reward in 1969.

There are some women who just never learn how to be good mothers-in-law. They interfere in the marriages of their children too much. Also, there are mothers-in-law who help the marriages' of their children.

It is not always possible for one to avoid trouble in a family. Jesus said, "Think not I am come to bring peace on the earth: I came not to bring peace but a sword. For I am come to set a man at variance against his father, and the daughter against her mother, and the daughter in law against the mother in law and a man's foes shall be they of his own household" (Matthew 10:34-36).

*To set at variance* is from Greek *dichasai* which means "To cut asunder, disunite." It's figurative meaning is "to set at variance," or "to make hostile."

It is obvious in the context of Matthew 10 that Jesus meant that even within a family there would be cases where some would accept his teaching and some would not. Such a difference of attitude would cause disunity.

Jesus is the Prince of Peace, but he is not a peace at any price prince!

Those who accept the teaching of the Saviour have peace among themselves but they may be at variance with many, even in their own families, who do not accept the truth. But those who accept the Lord are not to forsake him for the sake of those even in their own families who reject Jesus. That is why Jesus said, "He that loveth father or mother more than me is not worthy of me, and he that loveth son or daughter more than me is not worthy of me" (Matthew 10:37).

It could be that in a case where there is trouble that involves a mother-in-law, the mother-in-law would be right. She may be the one to stand for the truth!

The gospel is powerful enough to make all mothers-in-law and all daughters-in-law and all people to be good people. All people following the gospel is the only way all people will ever get along with each other.

It seems that some mothers-in-law do not highly

esteem their sons-in-law. It is reported that a woman made a set of pillow cases for her daughter and son-in-law. She embroidered HERS on one, and ITS on the other!

## Blindness

A Christian friend of mine, Ervin Nesbitt, told me that when he was a boy he had a blind mule named Frank.

In the pasture where Frank grazed, there was a big sink-hole. One day Ervin was in a swimming hole and could see a bunch of boys trying to get poor, blind Frank to walk into the sink-hole. Ervin saw the mule headed for the sink-hole and shouted: "Frank, come here boy." The blind beast responded to his master's voice immediately and turned toward the swimming hole and away from the sink-hole.

There are several lessons which I see in this true story. These are the following:

1. Some boys carry their "fun" too far. It has never been funny to me to see an animal mistreated; especially one that was handicapped. It is bad enough for an animal to be abused, but some people abuse other people trying to have fun. This is going too far to have fun.

I heard of a case where boys in a dormitory in a Christian College were "having fun" by throwing soft drinks bottles in a hall. A boy stuck his head out of the door of his room and a bottle hit him in his head and killed him. That was not any fun!

2. The mischeivous boys in the pasture were trying to get poor blind Frank into trouble. There are nearly always some who are trying to get other people into trouble. Solomon wrote about some who could not sleep unless they did mischief and caused someone to fall! (Proverbs 4:16) Imagine one being so mean that he would have to take sleeping pills if he did not cause others to get into trouble!

3. Blind Frank did not see what he was about to get

into when Ervin called for him. But Frank was a blind mule! He never even knew what he was about to get into.

Many people who are not literally blind are so blind in judgment and lacking in discernment that they do not see what they are getting into, and some go right on into trouble, woes, and horrible experiences even when someone is calling them and warning them.

In the gospel, God is calling us all trying to keep us out of "sink-holes" of trouble and trying to regulate and direct our lives so we won't have to endure horrible consequences of sins. However, many are not as smart as that blind mule was. It is hard to outsmart a good mule if you give him half a chance!

4. Frank obeyed his master. People need to obey their master, Jesus Christ. There is no way of calculating how much grief one escapes and avoids even in this world by obeying Jesus. By obeying Jesus we can also avoid eternal woe (2 Thessalonians 1:7-9).

Children can avoid much trouble and disappointment by obeying their parents.

Charles Coil told me he could recall many times that he would have avoided much trouble had he obeyed his Dad. He said that one time his Dad had told him to stay in a church-house, but he did not obey his Dad and by his going out of the church-house he got into a fight and caused his whole family to get into trouble.

Charles said he did not obey his Dad on another ocassion and he left a crowd at a ball game and a man pulled a knife on him. The man had just had a fight and said to Charles, "The last fellow I showed this knife to ran like a turkey. What are you going to do?" Charles said "Run like a turkey." That is what he did!

5. Those mischievous boys were taking advantage of poor, blind Frank. Unfortunately, people take advan-

tage of other people.

Mark Train told about a case that he felt was one of the meanest deeds on record. He felt a rock blasting company took advantage of one of its employees. He said the employee was packing powder into a hole with a crowbar getting it ready to blast the rock. The powder exploded while the fellow was packing it and sent the man and his crowbar out of sight. Mark said it was reported that the man and the crowbar came back in good shape in fifteen minutes and the man went back to work. His company took undue advantage of him by docking his pay for losing fifteen minutes.

Like so many of Mark's stories, one might have some doubts about whether or not it was a true story, but it does illustrate the meaness of men!

## He Wanted To Be Helpful

James Long told me a story about brother H.R. Gibson, Sr. (of Gibson Discount Centers).

Brother Gibson is a splendid Christian man who has been very successful as a business man. One reason he has been successful is that he has a good sense of humor.

Brother Gibson, like so many of the rest of us grew up in a rural area. (People in my home town of about 1500 people used to refer to those of us who did not live in that "city" as country people!)

Brother Gibson tells in a book he has written about an experience he and a friend had when he was a boy in Oklahoma. He and this young friend were riding a mule as they hunted swamp rabbits. (When I grew up a swamp rabbit sold for a dime. We thought that was good money for a rabbit. I have sold them for that.)

Brother Gibson and his friend got off the mule to walk across the river that was frozen over so they could hunt beyond the river. They left the mule and proceeded over the ice. When they were about half way across the river, they heard a noise and turning around they saw that mule right behind them. Soon the ice broke, and the boys went down into that cold river!

The mule managed to place his feet on a log and finally got safely on the river's bank. The boys also got out.

That mule was like some people he did not want to be left out of anything. That kind of attitude can get a lot of people in serious trouble!

You can't really tell what a mule is thinking or what he may do. Maybe that Oklahoma mule just wanted to be helpful! He was helpful all right; he helped those boys get a good cold soaking! He endangered his own life and the life of the boys!

Sometimes people who mean to be helpful use poor judgment and little or no discretion, and cause no little commotion. "A good man sheweth favor, and lendeth: he will guide his affairs with discretion"(Psalms112:5).

One man's wife tried to be helpful when they were fishing. A stranger came on the scene and commented about the splendid string of fish the man had caught. The man's wife said "If you think that is a nice display, you should look at all those he put in the weeds." The man had caught too many, and the stranger was a game warden!

## Hardeman Trained Mules Too!

Mules have been involved in the lives of some very famous people. I have been told that the name of David, king of Israel is in the Bible more than any other name. He owned a mule (1 Kings 1:33,38,44).

Even our Lord Jesus Christ made his triumphant entry into Jerusalem just before crucifixion riding on a beast that is of the same *kind* to which a mule belongs (Matthew 21:1-7).

One of the most famous friends I have had was N.B. Hardeman. He was one of my teachers. He was one of the best preachers the Lord has had. Brother Hardeman rode a mule in Jerusalem while on a Bible Land's tour.

Those who knew N.B. Hardeman usually think of him as owner, trainer, and lover of fine horses. I lived close to his house and barn and used to enjoy watching him ride his fine horses, especially his famous mare, Maid of Cotton.

What many may not realize is that brother Hardeman trained mules before he trained preachers. Remembering some of the experiences of the years I spent sitting at his feet, I can observe that training mules was probably an easier job than trying to train some of the preachers who attended his classes!

Mrs. Worth B. (Mary Nelle) Powers (one of brother's Hardeman's daughters) and James Marvin Powell wrote a book about brother Hardeman entitled: N.B.H. On pages 42 through 44 they tell of brother Hardeman's experiences with horses and mules. His father, Dr. John Bellefont Hardeman was a lover of fine horses. So brother N.B. said he inherited a love for horses.

Brother N.B. Hardeman also had considerable experience driving oxen hauling cotton and other products to market. One fall he hauled sixty-three bales of cotton to Coffee Landing on the Tennessee River taking three bales on each trip.

Sister Powers and brother Powell report that in his young years when brother Hardeman was not with the oxen he spent much time "breaking" and riding mules and yearlings. It seems it did not matter whether he was "breaking" young mules or yearlings or how wild and untamed they were.

Young Hardeman frequently rode a small "tow-headed" mule. On one trip on this mule the mule was moving fast and came to a creek and stopped suddenly. Hardeman went over the mule's ears into the middle of the creek!

Included in brother Hardeman's early schooling was his attending an entire session at Morris Chapel, Tennessee. He rode the three miles daily on a two-year-old black mule named Dolly.

I remember brother Hardeman's referring to mules. He would say that training a child involved the child's receiving the training. He said "You can't train a mule unless the mule is willing to receive the training."

Indeed the Bible teaches that children have a responsibility to receive the training of parents.

Solomon said, "Train up a child in the way he should go; and when he is old, he will not depart from it" (Proverbs 22:6). One might fail to train up his child by not teaching him properly and by not setting the proper example. However, he also might fail to train a child because the child would fail to accept or receive the training.

In the *first* chapter of Proverbs and in many chapters following there is great emphasis on the responsibility of children to receive the proper training. For an example, Proverbs 1:4 says that the purpose of the Book of Proverbs is "To give subtilty to the simple, to the young man knowledge and discretion." Then the text says "A wise man will hear and will increase learning."

In Proverbs 1:8 the instruction is, "My son, hear the instruction of thy father, and forsake not the law of thy mother." Similiar instruction and admonition is given to children in Proverbs 1:10,15; 2:1; 3:1-4,11,21; 4:1,20; 5:1-7; 6:1-20; 7:1,2,24,etc.

It is utter nonsense to say that parents have all the responsibility in training their children. Children are responsible to receive the proper training parents diligently try to give them. If they refuse to receive it, they will not be trained properly. God will bring the young into judgment for their deeds. (Ecclesiastes 11:9,10)

"Hear, ye children, the instruction of a father, and attend to know understanding" (Proverbs 4:1). Do not forget this passage and many others like it when you interpret Proverbs 22:6.

Yes, brother Hardeman was right, training mules involved both the trainer and the mule. And training children involves the wills of both those who do the training and those whom they try to train.

"Hear me now therefore, O ye children, and depart not from the words of my mouth" (Proverbs 5:7).

## Mind Changing Experiences

An elder in the church in Missouri told Charles Coil a true mule story and Charles has presented it to me as follows:

"A St. Louis man came to southern Missouri and put in a factory in a quiet little hill town. The factory owner was not only rich but was a rough talking, hard drinking, over-bearing brawler accustomed to having his own way.

"One day his chauffered limousine went whirling down a back road near the little hill town when the driver overtook an old farmer riding a mule.

The mule had a collar and harness around his neck with the trace chains hooked over the harness. A feed sack was tied to the harness and a handle of some sort stuck out of the sack.

"Sign of toil on the mule and the overalls and old black hat of the man indicated they were returning from work in either fields or woods.

"When the driver had to veer around the mule, the impatient St. Louisan, became angry. He ordered to the chauffeur to stop the car and he jumped out and ran back to meet the mule rider. 'Get down old man,' he roared, 'and I will teach you a lesson. Next time you will get out of the road when you see me coming!' (Parts of the conversation are not repeatable.)

"Both the mule rider and the mule observed the fierce challenger with mild interest. The old farmer just spoke one word. 'Alright,' he said, as he slid down from the mule. However, as he came off the mule, he pulled a double-bit chopping axe from the feed sack!

"The roaring ceased. Road gravel flew from the patent leather shoes of the city man, and a few seconds later from the tires of his big limousine. The mule and the farmer watched him go and then resumed their unhurried journey home to supper."

The foregoing illustrates how one so determined to do something can have his mind changed by circumstances! It reminds me of the story about the man who disliked a preacher because of things the preacher had preached. As the preacher was riding out of town in his buggy, the man who hated him was standing in the road and stopped the mule pulling the buggy and told the preacher, "Get out of the buggy, I'm gonna whip you."

The preacher said, "I always like to pray before entering any endeavor, so I'd like to pray first." Whereupon the other man said, "Get your praying done."

The preacher prayed something like this, "Lord, you know how strong I am, and how uncontrollable my strength is. You know when I choked Junior Bills to death, I lost control of my muscles. You remember I am sure the time John Bush attacked me and I beat his brains out against that brick wall. And Lord, you know I really did not want to so badly cripple Caleb Stoker the time he tried to abuse me. Now Lord help me to deal with this man properly."

When the preacher had closed his prayer, his enemy was running fast from the scene. Something seemed to change his mind!

The foregoing is not related to encourage preachers or anyone else to be brutal or to pray like that, but it does illustrate how one so determined to do something can have his mind changed.

There are times when any one of us needs to change his mind.

1. Those who are determined in their belief that the

Bible is not God's word, need to change their minds to believing the Bible is God's word. Such a change of mind would be incentive to change from living in rebellion against God to living in submission to the God who loves them and wants them to live so they can live with him eternally.

2. Some who say they believe the Bible is God's word seem determined to depend on their feelings instead of what the Bible says. They need to change their minds and begin to carefully study and see what God requires of them instead of depending on their feelings. One feels good if he does God's will. But, doing God's will, not his feelings, is the proof he is right.

Some feel they are right religiously who do not even know God's will. One's feelings can deceive him. Everyone needs to study the Bible carefully and learn God's will and do it.

3. Members of the Lord's church who seem set on living so that they bring reproach on Christ and his church, and "crucify to themselves the Son of God afresh, and put him to an open shame" (Hebrews 6:6) should change their minds and lives so they could be lights shining in a dark world of sin, "holding forth the word of life" (Philippians 2:15,16).

## Disrespect, Greed, and Selfishness

Hubert (Stubby) George is the preacher for the church in Double Springs, Alabama.

While I was with Stubby in a series of meetings he told me several good mule stories which remind me of many important lessons. Here is one of the stories he told me.

A man died and someone went to school to tell his two boys the sad news. When they were told of their daddy's death, one of them said to the other, "I want first chance on Pa's gray mule."

It would seem that boy cared very little for his Pa, and he was quite greedy and selfish.

Some children are not as respectful of their parents as they should be. Paul predicted that children would be disobedient to parents, which means a lack of respect. (2 Timothy 3:1,2)

Some of the saddest stories are stories about children fussing over the material things left to them by their parents. Jesus was asked by a man to speak to the man's brother about the brother dividing an inheritance properly. Jesus told him that he was not a judge or divider over them. Then he told them that they should beware of covetousness because "a man's life consisteth not in the abundance of the things which he possesseth" (Luke 12:13-15). Money and other material possessions are not wrong, but there is more to life than these!

Greed and covetousness have caused a big part of the woes of history.

An Arab proverb says, "Covetousness has for its mother unlawful desire, for its daughter injustice, and for its friends violence."

Some elderly are covetous and greedy. Cicero said,

"Avarice in old age is foolish; for what can be more ab-
surd than to increase our provisons for the road, the
nearer we approach our journey's end."

"Two things are difficult
   for man to do;
Tis to be selfish,
   and be honest too."

## Two Kentucky Mules

This author preached in a series of meetings several years ago with the Clements St. Church of Christ in Paducah, Kentucky. John Starks was the preacher for that church at that time. Two of my old friends, Charles Hays, and R. H. Penn were the elders.

My Margie and I lived in Paducah during 1953, 1954 and through most of 1955. I preached during those years for the Murrell Boulevard Church of Christ which is now known as Central.

While preaching in this series at Clements St. Church, Margie and I resided with Harold and Pat Wood and their son Michael. We enjoyed the tremendous hospitality of this splendid Christian home. (Harold is a gospel preacher, and I got him his first appointment in 1959. He has been preaching ever since.)

Harold took me to see an old friend of mine, brother L. D. Houser, a faithful man of God. Brother Houser is a cousin of Frank E. Wood, Harold's father who is deceased.

After brother Houser showed us his little mare mule, Jenny Bell, he pulled her bridle off and in perfectly proper mule manners she demonstrated her ability to wallow in the dirt!

Brother Houser purchased Jenny Bell only after she proved herself. Before he agreed to buy her he hooked her to the biggest plow he had, and put it in the hardest ground he could find. Jenny Bell truly proved herself, and the trade was made.

The Bible teaches that some men were appointed in congregations to serve in a special way under the elders as deacons. The qualifications for deacons are found in 1 Timothy Chapter 3. One of the qualifications it seems is not noticed very well. It is: "And let these also frist be proved; then let them use the office of a deacon, being found blameless" (1 Timothy 3:10).

Men should not be appointed to be deacons unless they first prove themselves by their demonstrating dependability, trustworthiness, faithfulness to the Lord, love for the truth, love for the church, and love for souls! A man needs to pull a big plow in hard ground, so to speak, before being appointed as a deacon!

Being a deacon is a serious work fraught with eternal consequences. Being a deacon does not just involve painting the church building or fixing the plumbing, etc. Being a deacon involves growing into boldness in the faith, and faithfulness in all things. (1 Timothy 3:11,13)

All the children in the community where brother Houser lived enjoyed riding Jenny Bell. One trait of this little mule was very noticeable when she entertained the children, or at any other time. She would not go near a mole hole. She would make great efforts to avoid such. A mole hole spelled trouble to her.

Harold Wood wisely observed about this trait of Jenny Bell's, "You know, Basil, we all many times as Christians could stay out of trouble and problems if we too were more cautious of many things, including the

wiles of the devil which are the many methods the devil uses to tempt us (Ephesians 6:11)." How true!

Clarence Le Neave is the song director at Clements St. Church. While in that series of meetings with that church my Margie and I enjoyed the hospitality of several of the families of the church including a meal and fellowship in the home of Clarence and his good wife, Edna. They live near the home of Alben W. Barkley who served as Vice President of the United States. When we lived in Paducah we lived near Mr. Barkley and we have often regreted that we did not visit him.

Mr. Barkley's home is being developed into a shrine.

Brother Le Neave said he heard Mr. Barkley give a report when he was Vice President on how many "wings" (airplanes) various nations had. Someone asked him how many wings the United States had and Mr. Barkley replied, "I do not know; they have not told me; I suppose it is a secret."

In his inimitable manner, Mr. Barkley then told a true story. He said he was reminded of one of his experiences when he lived at Wheel near Mayfield, Kentucky. He said he was on his way to Mayfield in a wagon pulled by his big mule and his little mule. As he was passing a pasture he saw a mule that looked just like his big mule. He went to the owner and bought that mule. After he got the mule home he discovered it was blind. He went and asked the former owner if he knew the mule was blind. The man said, "Yes." Mr. Barkley asked why he did not tell him the mule was blind. The man replied, "The man who sold the mule to me did not tell me the mule was blind; I thought it was a secret."

It is not wrong to keep secrets. But it is wrong to withhold information that needs to be revealed in order for a trade or deal to be fair. Withholding such information is a species of lying. One can lie in some circumstances by not saying what he should say.

One cannot guarantee an old car when he trades it. There might be something wrong with a car of which one is not aware when trading it. But if one is aware of a serious defect in a car or any other possession he trades or sells he should tell the one proposing to trade with him about it, and not keep it a secret!

## Afraid When No Danger

My Dad, W.R. Overton (deceased) of Weakley County, Tennessee had many experiences with mules. Some of these were frightening, and even injurious to him. Others were amusing.

Forty and more years ago, when we went to Greenfield in the Owensboro wagon pulled by mules, I was always somewhat tense when a steam locomotive came into town pulling a train on the Illinois Central Railroad. Our mules were not at all fond of those giant black, smoking, whistling, and puffing engines. They especially disliked that puffing of the black smoke! Sometimes the mules would try to run away! A boy that has not been with mules on main street on Saturday afternoon when a big crowd of people was in town, has missed an experience that defies description!

Those mules were really in no danger when a locomotive pulled a train through town close to them. Those of us in the wagon were in danger because of the way the mules reacted. The mules sensed they were in great danger when they were perfectly safe. They could have gone to sleep right by the railroad track and been unharmed.

Some people are afraid when there is no need to be alarmed. Others do not become alarmed or concerned when they need to.

Dad said that one day he had been plowing with his mules and they had fretted him so much he decided to leave them for a spell and let them calm down. While he was away, instead of calming down they ran away with the plow, and the plow caught a piece of American wire fence on which a good crop of beans was growing. The wire, bean vines and all were pulled out. Such a stunt was not unusual for mules!

This true story illustrates how that some things are done at the wrong time. Had the bean crop already been harvested, and had my father wanted to clear the ground in the garden, what those mules did would have been a good deed.

People also do things at the most inappropriate times. It is reported that a barber was very zealous about trying to save the lost. He was about to shave a man; he had his razor fixed ready to start the job, and then he earnestly looked into the eyes of the man he was about to shave and enthusiastically asked him, "Are you prepared to die"?

## Drive Or Draw?

Jesse Tubbs, who was one of my students at International Bible College told me about a farmer trying for some time to run his mules into a fenced lane that led to a barn. With great effort the man was unable to drive the mules into the narrow lane.

The farmer's wife walked into the pasture with a bucket and got in front of the mules and walked toward the lane holding the bucket in view of the mules. She walked slowly and the mules followed her into the lane and on to the barn!

This story illustrates how we can sometimes lead when we cannot drive. Much time and effort have been wasted by some who have tried in vain to drive others.

Even God does not drive; he draws. One cannot read in the Bible about the driving power of the Lord, but Jesus said no one could come to him unless the Father draw (lead) him first. He then explained that the Father draws or leads people by their hearing and learning of him. (John 6:44,45)

Elders of a congregation should not be "drivers," but leaders. By their examples they should draw the flock. Elders are told by the Holy Spirit not to be lords over God's heritage. (1 Peter 5:3)

I have known elders who seemed to think they had to show their authority in some way.

"Remember them that have the rule over you, who have spoken unto you the word of God, whose faith follow, considering the end of your conversation" (Hebrews 13:7). It seems that the holy writer referred to elders in this verse as those who have "the rule over you." In verse 17 of the same chapter, the writer said, "Obey them that have the rule over you . . . " In verse

24 he said "Salute them that have the rule over you . . . "

In each of these verses "rule over you" is a translation of some form of the Greek word *hegomai* which is defined: "to lead the way; to take the lead; to be the chief; to preside; govern, rule; a leader; a guide.

Undoubtedly, elders have authority, and they should exercise it when necessary, but not just for the sake of exercising it and thus be "lords over God's heritage." But they should "lead the way," in the Lord's work. They should not be drivers," but leaders!

Those mules that the farmer's wife led to the barn with a bucket were very much like most of us humans. With great effort we may be driven relunctantly, but we prefer to be lead!

# Would Not Speak

October 7 through November 6, 1976 I was in the Veterans Hospital in Birmingham, Alabama. I had open-heart surgery October 20, 1976. Many others were there for heart surgery. Among them was Paul Teaford of Walker County, Alabama. His wife Ruth told me a mule story which should remind us all of a very important matter.

Ruth said a farmer was plowing. A mule was pulling the plow and the man had great difficulty getting the mule to turn at the corners. He pulled the plow line vigorously and could barely get the beast to turn.

A man saw the plowman having such a struggle getting the mule to turn, and he noticed that the farmer was not saying anything in the struggle to get the animal to turn as he should.

The gentlemen observing the strange scene said to the farmer, "Sir, if you speak to the mule and say "Gee" when you want him to turn right, and say "Haw" when you want him to turn left, he will likely respond much more quickly and your job will be much easier."

The farmer replied, "I have not spoken to that mule in six months!"

There are times when it is best not to speak any words. Someone has said it is better on some ocassions not to say anything and let people *think* you are a fool than it is to open your mouth and remove all doubt.

While I was in the hospital I heard a patient tell a very ugly and nasty story while we were eating a meal. I told him I did not appreciate it. He did not get mad, but another patient did not like what I said and would not speak to me.

Not speaking to another is a sign of immaturity. That farmer surely made matters much worse for himself because he would not speak to his mule.

One might overdo his speaking to others and be branded as a nuisance or a bore. Abraham Lincoln said of a lawyer he knew, "He can compress the most words into the smallest ideas of any man I ever saw."

I heard about a young man who was telling about the death of his daddy. Someone asked him, "What were you pa's last words?" He replied, "He didn't have any, Ma was there." Such is not characteristic of all wives. Such could be said of some husbands too. Some spouses become known as "speaker of the house!"

Sometimes one needs to speak; at other times he needs to be silent. "Wherefore my beloved brethren, let every man be swift to hear, slow to speak, slow to wrath" (James 1:9).

"A soft answer turneth away wrath; but grievous words stir up anger. The tongue of the wise useth knowledge aright; but the mouth of fools poureth out foolishness" (Proverbs 15:1,2).

When you need to, talk to your mule! Speak to people and be friendly, but don't do all the talking around your associates! "There is that speaketh like the piercing of the sword, but the tongue of the wise is health" (Proverbs 12:18).

## Prayed Then "Cussed"

I heard my father tell about an experience his grandfather and his great uncle had with a team of mules. They were driving the mules to a wagon and they had to cross a stream. The wagon stuck in the bed of the river and it seemed as if the mules were going to drown. It was reported that the two men prayed to get out, and to save the mules and the wagon. After much anxiety, prayer, and excitement they finally persuaded the mules to get out of the river with the wagon and all was well.

After getting on dry ground and being safe and secure, it is said the two men began to "cuss" the mules.

I do not suppose these were the only ones who have prayed to God for help and then acted very inconsistently afterward.

When we have asked God to help us in our trials and difficulties we should do our best to live as he wants us to.

As God's children we should call on God for help when we become involved in difficulties, but we should pray at all times.

"Pray without ceasing" (1 Thessalonians 5:17).

"Without ceasing" of this command to Christians is from the Greek word *adeialeiptos* which is defined: "Unceasingly, by an unvarying practice." Obviously, Paul did not command Christians to pray without ceasing in the sense that we can do nothing but pray, because that would be impossible! He meant that we are to pray regularly, or as an unvarying practice, and not just when we get in a difficult predicament!

In the next verse Paul said, "In everything give thanks: for this is the will of God in Christ Jesus concerning you" (1 Thessalonians 5:18).

Our prayers for help should be followed by thanksgiving for God's help. Recently I asked God's forgiveness because I felt I had not expressed my thanks to him as much as I should have for all he brought me through in heart surgery. It is so easy to fail to thank God for all he does for us. He does much for us and gives us many things for which we do not ask him!

There is so very much for which we should thank him without ceasing, or regularly!

Even Jesus thanked God for hearing him. When he was about to raise Lazarus from the dead he lifted up his eyes and said, "Father I thank thee that thou hast heard me" (John 11:41). If our Lord Jesus by whom God created all things (Colossians 1:15,16) was thankful that his Father heard him, how much more should we feeble, mortal creatures be thankful when God has heard us!